Susan Campbell's search for an old-fashioned walled kitchen garden which was still being kept up and run on traditional lines came to an end when she heard about Cottesbrooke.

The three-acre kitchen garden there was still being maintained as it was in 1930, while the design of the garden seemed to have changed little since the late nineteenth century. Muscats, figs and peaches flourished in the numerous heated greenhouses and frames, and the store-rooms were filled with produce. It represented the perfect kitchen garden time-capsule, preserving the gardening traditions of the past alongside modern horticultural techniques.

The book is in the form of a diary for the year 1984-1985. The chapters chronicle the work in the garden, month by month. Susan Campbell describes the weather, the flowers and pot plants, the fruit and vegetables being sent up to the house, the comings and goings, the planting and the harvesting. The numerous evocative photographs and line drawings complement the text and build up a unique record of the annual cycle of digging, weeding, pricking out, watering, potting on, planting, pruning and picking. It is a book to arouse the admiration and envy of fellow gardeners and to fascinate social historians and all those who enjoy the nostalgia of a more expansive, but now vanished way of life.

Susan Campbell is a writer and illustrator. She has published many books including *Poor Cook, Family Cook* and *Bumper Cook* (all with Caroline Conran), *Cheap Eats, Guide to Good Food Shops, Cook's Companion, English Cookery Old and New* and *A Calendar of Gardeners' Lore* (Century). She has written for the *Sunday Times, Sunday Telegraph* and *Observer* magazines, *Time Out, Harpers & Queen* and *Taste*. She has two grown-up sons and divides her time between London and Hampshire.

Dedicated to the memory
of Catherine Macdonald–Buchanan

COTTESBROOKE

An English Kitchen Garden

Compiled and Illustrated By

S U S A N   C A M P B E L L

With Photographs By

H U G H   P A L M E R

Salem House Publishers

Topsfield, Massachusetts

FIRST PUBLISHED IN THE UNITED STATES
BY SALEM HOUSE PUBLISHERS, 1987
462 BOSTON STREET, TOPSFIELD, MA 01983

LIBRARY OF CONGRESS CATALOGING IN PUBLICATION DATA
Campbell, Susan, 1931-
Cottesbrooke: the diary of a traditional kitchen garden.

Includes index.
1. Vegetable gardening – England – Northamptonshire.
2. Fruit-culture – England – Northamptonshire.
3. Cottesbrooke Kitchen Garden (England) I. Palmer,
Hugh. II. Title.
SB322.C36 1987   635'.09425'5   87-4495
ISBN 0-88162-249-4

DESIGNED BY BOB HOOK

SET BY SX COMPOSING LTD

PRINTED AND BOUND IN GREAT BRITAIN

CONTENTS

INTRODUCTION

I first heard about the kitchen gardens at Cottesbrooke, in the East Midlands, in the spring of 1984. At that time I was gathering material for a history of kitchen gardening in Great Britain. I had already spent three years investigating the remains of literally hundreds of old walled kitchen gardens all over the country, but I had more or less given up the hope that my researches might actually lead to the discovery of a garden that was still being run to its full capacity in the traditional manner.

This traditional garden would be enclosed by high walls, with possibly an orchard alongside. It would have hothouses capable of supplying its owner with figs, grapes, peaches, melons and nectarines, as well as forced vegetables and exotic pot plants. It would have potting sheds, vegetable and fruit stores, and a work-force big enough to keep a fair-sized household in fruit, cut flowers, vegetables and indoor plants all the year round.

Gardens like this were the rule, rather than the exception in all proper country establishments before the Second World War. The economic changes brought about by that war put paid to most of them; a few survived into the Fifties, but by the Seventies even those survivors had disappeared thanks to the ever-rising costs of fuel and labour, and the increasing availability of imported garden produce.

The gardens I had looked at had ranged in size from the single acre gardens which are typical of a modest country house to gardens of ten or twenty acres designed for the use of ducal or even regal establishments. All were defunct. Some had been completely abandoned and were now covered in weeds, with fruit trees growing wild and glasshouses in ruins. Some had been ploughed up and planted with agricultural crops. Others had been converted into paddocks or *manèges* for horses (walled gardens are apparently well suited for the training of horses). Some of the largest, like those at Blenheim, Welbeck and Holkham, had been converted into garden centres. Horticulture was still being carried out in them, but it was hardly the kind I was looking for. Many more were being used as nurseries for Christmas trees, another purpose to which old walled kitchen gardens are well suited, as their

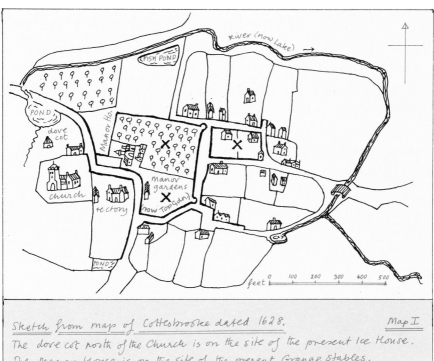

Sketch from map of Cottesbrooke dated 1628. Map I

The dove cot north of the Church is on the site of the present Ice House.

The Manor House is on the site of the present Grange Stables.

The Pond to the north of the dove cot is now dry and the present road passes to the south of it and the Ice House. (see Map II)

The present orchard and kitchen gardens, with the frame yard, lie roughly in the areas marked 'X'.

strong, high walls protect the young plants and give security against both animal and human predators.

It was a depressing situation, but occasionally I came across the owner of an old kitchen garden who, while unable to keep it going entirely as it was originally intended, did at least manage to preserve the historical spirit of the place. Many of these owners contacted me after I had given an interview on the radio about old kitchen gardens; among them were the curators of a large country house museum and park in the West Midlands who wanted advice on the possible restoration of some of their kitchen garden buildings. It was while I was visiting them that a young graduate on the museum staff told me about Cottesbrooke. The garden there, I was assured, was still being run as it used to be fifty years ago and more. The head gardener was a distant relation of my informant. He had lent her section of the museum a grape bottle, an object which I had read about in late nineteenth-century gardening books but had never seen. Apparently there were dozens more of these

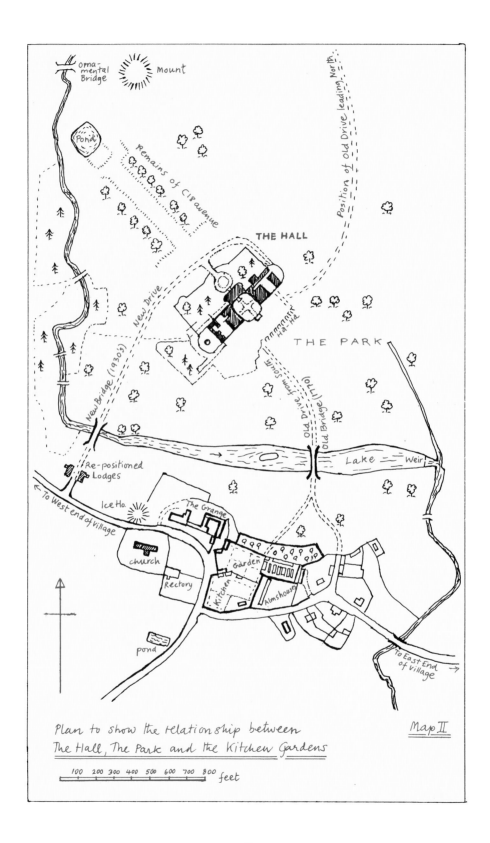

Ornamental Bridge

Mount

Pond

Remains of C18 avenue

Position of Old Drive leading North

THE HALL

New Drive

Ha-Ha

THE PARK

New Bridge (1930s)

Old Drive (from South)

Old Bridge (1770)

Lake

Weir

Re-positioned Lodges

Ice Ho.

To West end of Village

The Grange

church

Garden

Rectory

Kitchen

Almshouses

pond

To East End of Village

Plan to show the relationship between The Hall, The Park and the Kitchen Gardens

Map II

100 200 300 400 500 600 700 800 feet

bottles at Cottesbrooke. The vinery there produced a great many grapes which the head gardener wished to keep as far into the winter as possible, but he was doubtful if any of his grapes were suitable varieties for keeping by the old grape-bottle system.

This in itself was enough to make me want to visit the garden at Cottesbrooke, but on learning that everything there, including frames and hothouses, two acres of walled garden, an orchard, a fruit store, a root store and a gardener's office, was still in use and daily providing its owner with all the garden produce a fairly large household could need, I began to suspect that I had at last found the very garden I was looking for. The more I learnt about it, the more interesting it became. The first time I saw it I thought it was such a remarkable survival of the recent past that it really merited a book to itself.

The owner of these gardens is an elderly lady, recently widowed. Nothing in the running of the gardens or her house has changed much since she and her family first went to live there in 1935.

Earlier history reveals that Cottesbrooke has never been much of a place for the chopping and changing of ownership either. The manor is mentioned in Domesday. It was the home of a family called Buttivillar, Butevileyn or Boutevileins for over three centuries and went through various owners between 1499 and 1638, being shared at one time by seven sisters. It was bought by John Langham in 1638. His grandson built the present Hall between 1702 and 1712. The Langhams lived here until 1911 when, to quote the present owner, 'They ran out of money'. The estate was then bought by a descendant of the railway millionaire Thomas Brassey. The Brasseys lived here for only twenty-four years, but in that short time they made many changes, especially in the gardens. Between 1911 and the outbreak of the First World War in 1914 they employed the firm of Messenger to build the range of hothouses, frames and garden buildings that are still in use today, and the Edwardian architect Robert Weir Schultz redesigned the pleasure gardens immediately surrounding the house. The remains of an extensive formal early eighteenth-century garden can still be seen to the north-west of the house, but by the late eighteenth century such a garden was already old-fashioned. It was probably abandoned and made to look more natural at that time, with the landscaping of the park. It was completely forgotten by the Victorian era, when parterres and carpet bedding would have been the style.

The present owner has changed the early twentieth-century Brassey gardens very little. The biggest alteration has been to the main drive which was re-sited in the Thirties to the north-west of the church, so that it approaches the house on its northern side instead of on the southern side, as it used to. The late eighteenth-century lodge-gates which originally stood a couple of miles away, high up on the main road to the west, were also moved at this time to mark the entrance of the new drive.

However, it is the Langhams who laid the heaviest stamp on the Cottesbrooke estate. They owned it for 272 years, from 1639 to 1911. From the eighteenth century onwards they lived very quietly here, prominent in local affairs but not, apparently, much concerned with matters of national importance. They were connected by marriage to the Christies of Glyndebourne and are famous for little else except that by building a house in London in 1814 the tenth baronet gave his name to Langham Place; it is opposite Broadcasting House. Their country mansion, known to the village as 'The Hall', was built by Francis Smith of Warwick for the fourth baronet, Sir John Langham, in 1702; it was finished in 1711. It is a handsome brick house in the Queen Anne style set in a pretty park. It stands at some distance from the village and the original manor house, which was situated opposite the church.

John Langham had bought the manor of Cottesbrooke half at a time, in 1638 and 1642, for £35,000. It was his drive and ambition that created the fortune with which his descendants were to build the Hall, and create the park which we see today. He was born in 1584 into a poor family that lived locally. The legend is that his mother was cruel to him and he ran away, resolving not to return until he was rich. The story is a little like that of Dick Whittington, 200 years before him. He became a grocer in the City of London, and is later described as a 'Turkey merchant'. By the age of 35 he had married the widowed sister of a fellow merchant; she was to bear him fifteen children and to die aged 52. He became associated with the East India Company and was later a Court Assistant to the Levant Company which was, at the time, 'the most flourishing and beneficall company to the commonwealth of any in England'. The company's exports of lead, tin and wool to Constantinople, Aleppo and Smyrna were sufficient to pay for the currants, wines, oils, silks, cotton, carpets and spices that were brought back, and sufficient to make a fortune for John Langham. By 1634 he was Treasurer to the Levant Company. Four years later he was in a position to buy the manor of Cottesbrooke. In 1641 he became an Alderman of the Portsoken Ward in the City. From 1642 to 1643 he was the Sheriff of London and might well have become Lord Mayor, but these were troubled times. As a loyal supporter of the King, both before and during the Civil War, he was no friend to

Eighteenth century bridge in the Park

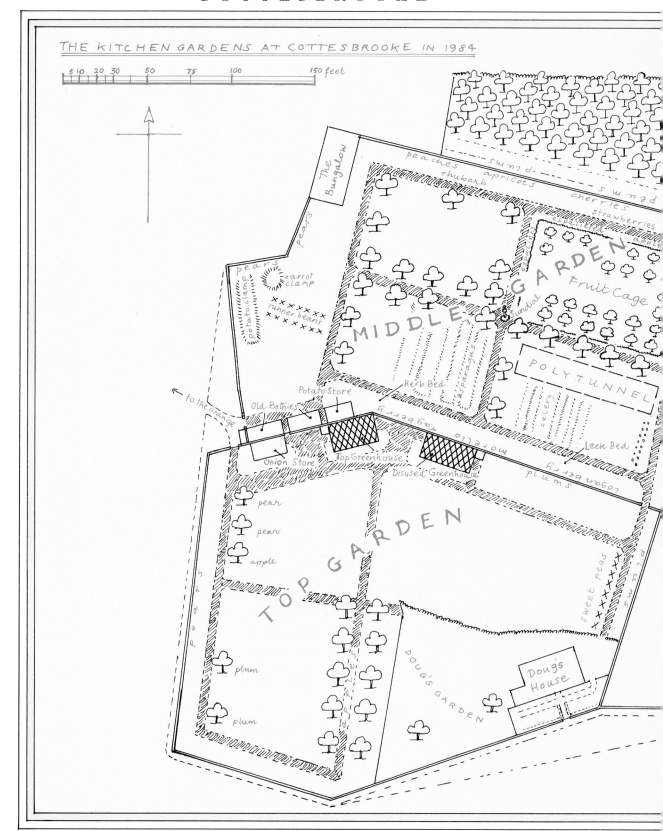

THE KITCHEN GARDENS AT COTTESBROOKE IN 1984

5 10 20 30   50   75   100   150 feet

The Bungalow

pears

pears

pears

peaches   apricots
rhubarb
s u m d
s u m a d
cherries
strawberries
espaliered apple

carrot clamp
potato clamp
runner beans

MIDDLE GARDEN

Fruit Cage

Sundial

POLY TUNNEL

asparagus

Herb Bed

celery

Leek Bed

Potato Store

Old Bothies

to the Grange

Onion Store

Top Greenhouse
Disused Greenhouse

raspberry
morello
raspberry
plums
loganberry

pear

pear

apple

TOP GARDEN

pears

plum

plum

apples

plums

sweet peas

Doug's House

DOUG'S GARDEN

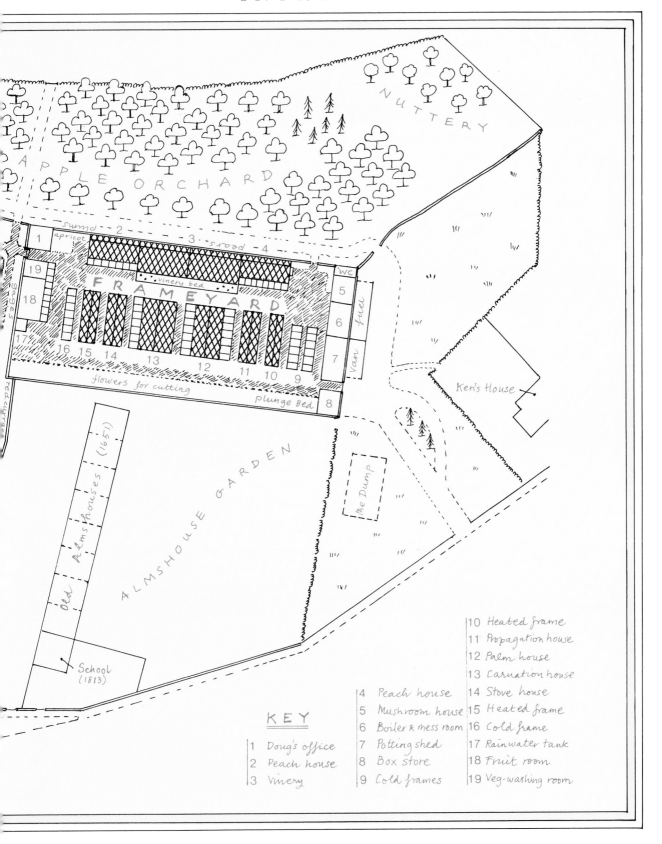

NUTTERY

APPLE ORCHARD

1

sumd - 2 - apricot

3 · pears · 4

vinery bed

FRAMEYARD

19

18

gages

17

16   15   14   13   12   11   10   9

flowers for cutting

plunge Bed

redcurrants

WC

5

6

Van fred

7

8

Ken's House

Old Almshouses (1651)

ALMSHOUSE GARDEN

The Dump

School (1813)

Parliament and in 1647, at the age of 63, he was imprisoned in the Tower with five other Aldermen. Two years later, and three months after the execution of Charles I, he was released. By 1654 he was the Governor of the Levant Company, and the Member of Parliament for London. In 1660 (now aged 76) he went to Holland as part of the deputation sent to bring Charles II back to England. In return for their support he and his son James were knighted in the May of that year. He was created a baronet in June. He died, not at Cottesbrooke, but at his City house in Bishopsgate on 13 May 1671.

John Langham established numerous charitable foundations both in his native county and in London. One of them, providing eight dwellings for six poor widows and two widowers over 60 and 'such as are past their daily labour and have no other support', was built in 1651 as a row of almshouses at Cottesbrooke. These still stand, with what remains of their acre of land, just behind the kitchen garden walls.

The manor house in the village in which both he and his first and second sons would have lived appears to have been either destroyed or allowed to tumble down some time after the grand new house was built by his grandson in its spacious park. The manor house gardens, however, survive in the form of today's kitchen gardens. A map of 1628 shows the old gardens on the very same, curiously-shaped site that the kitchen gardens and orchard occupy today. The park and gardens surrounding the mansion always were, and still are, purely ornamental. No part of them appears to have been used at any time for fruit or vegetables.

The kitchen gardens at Cottesbrooke are therefore older than the pleasure gardens and the mansion. They are possibly even older than I already know them to be. It seems probable that they have been in constant cultivation since 1628 – it could be longer.

There was some likelihood, then, that gardening traditions which I had only read about, or heard tell of from very old gardeners, still lived on in the 1980s and if they did, which were they? Horticultural techniques interested me as well. Modern techniques must have replaced many of the older ones, but which remained unchanged? And how did today's labour regulations affect a kitchen garden run on old-fashioned lines? I wanted to make a proper study of the place and the way it worked. To make this study I thought it ought to be visited at least once a month for at least one year. With the owner's kind permission and the head gardener's co-operation I therefore began this record in October 1984. I invited Hugh Palmer to be the photographer, and together we began to compile the written and pictorial diary which follows.

OCTOBER

Monday, 8 October 1984, our first visit to Cottesbrooke

Hugh and I have driven up the motorway from London and made our way to the heart of the East Midlands. The weather is typical of early October; it is, perhaps, one of the last fine, calm days we will have before winter sets in.

The countryside is still green; this part of the country is mainly farmland, both arable and pasture. There are many small rivers and brooks. Gentle hills fold round ancient hamlets and villages. We are near a famous Civil War battlefield. The houses and cottages are mostly built of local dark-ochre ironstone, or a mixture of stone, brick and cob. Many of their roofs are thatched, others are tiled with stone or slate.

On approaching Cottesbrooke we are bewildered by a network of lanes bordered with wide grass verges. The fields are bounded by noticeably substantial posts and rails or low, well-trimmed thorn hedges and ditches. Not a bramble or a strand of wire is to be seen, for this is one of the parts of England where the fox-hunting is of the very best. We are in 'the grass', not far from country that Mr Jorrocks described as 'the heaven of heavens'. It has been, since the 1770s, the stamping ground of countless dukes, earls, princes and, even, of an Austrian empress. This is a place that I have never visited before, but I know all about it, for as a child my reading consisted entirely of books on hunting and ponies and a paper called *Horse and Hound*. This, I tell Hugh who remains unimpressed, is country made famous by such names as The Pytchley, The Bicester and Warden Hill, The Fernie and The Grafton. As we drive past copses, coverts, rides and jumpable brooks, I can picture the landscape of a little later on in the year; with a pack of hounds in full cry, followed by huntsmen in pink, it will look exactly like a painting by Lionel Edwards, the artist I admired most when I was at boarding school.

Our arrival at Cottesbrooke is timed to coincide with the gardeners' mid-morning break at half-past ten. We are greeted by the head gardener and his wife at the door of a newish, plain but substantial house with a very tidy box hedge in front. This is the Gardens House, built just after the Second World War for the previous head gardener, who retired some eighteen months ago after twenty years in the post. Cottesbrooke's new head gardener

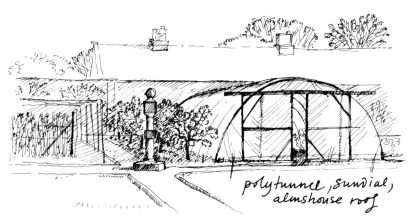

*polytunnel, sundial,
almshouse roof*

is always referred to by his surname by both his employer and his
staff, but I was at once invited to call him Doug. He is stocky, well
built and approaching 50. His voice has a West Midlands burr;
both he and his wife Joy are from Stoke-on-Trent. His father was a
coal-miner but, except for a spell in the regular army, Doug's
career has been gardening ever since he left school.

Joy gives us coffee in her spotless, cosy sitting room. The rest
of the garden staff have their break in the mess room. Doug's
house, as we can see from the windows, is right inside the kitchen
gardens, on the southern side of the walled garden which is known
as the Top Garden. (This is the one-acre garden that is shown on
the map of 1628 as a square with one corner sliced off.) Beyond the
western wall we can see the church tower and the rectory; on the
wall opposite there are two nineteenth-century greenhouses and,
just visible behind the high wall on the eastern side of the garden,
the roofs of the Alderman Langham's almshouses with 'Anno
Domini 1651' carved on the northern gable.

A wide cinder path runs beneath this wall. It is bordered by
blazing dahlias and leads to the second, slightly smaller walled
garden which is always referred to as the Middle Garden. (This is
the garden due east of the old manor house, shown as orchard on
the 1628 map.) But as if to remind us that we are in the second half
of the twentieth century, we are suddenly faced with an 85-foot
long, 9-foot high and 18-foot wide polythene tunnel. It looks like a
beached whale with its thick, shiny semi-transparent skin
stretched tightly over its hooped ribs. It occupies almost the whole
of one of the four quarters into which this otherwise traditionally
laid-out garden is divided. Another quarter is taken up by a large,
newly planted fruit cage. Each of the cross-walks of this garden is
lined with apple trees. Some are very old; others, in the form of
espaliered double-U's, are also newly planted. Where the paths
meet in the middle there is a curious pillar with a sundial on top. It
is decidedly Edwardian in style, and a doleful verse is engraved on
each of its four sides.

Both the Top and Middle Gardens are immaculately neat. Where it is vacant the ground is clean and newly dug, showing rich, crumbly dark earth. Cabbages, sprouts and kale stand in regimented lines; neat fan-trained fruit trees occupy every inch of the walls except where these trees are also newly planted and not yet fully grown into their spaces. A section of the eastern wall is devoted to cordoned red currants and gooseberries.

I had rather hoped that the paths here would be traditionally made of grass, cinders or gravel, with neat little edgings of box, but they are not. They are concrete; untraditional but practical, as befits paths in a garden that is, as I now see, not so much a romantic *potager* as a busy and productive working place. These paths are dry, weedless and clean, with dark-blue fired-clay edgings of a kind I've not seen before. The design is ingenious, the side nearest the bed is vertical to enable a spade to go straight downwards and the side nearest the path projects at an angle, below ground level.

Three-quarters of an acre of apple orchard and a small nuttery lie to the north of the Middle Garden. Beyond that is the park, dipping down to the river. The river was widened here by Alderman Langham's grandson when he began building the Hall in 1702. It now forms a lake about 600 yards long and 200 feet across at its widest point. The little stone bridge that was built in 1770 to carry an old drive across the park to the mansion, stands just below the kitchen gardens where the lake narrows slightly to form a waist. It has three elegant arches and a stone balustrade. We can just see the house through the park's handsome trees. It stands half a mile off on higher ground, four-square, remote and quietly imposing. Rather than face due north towards the square tower of Cottesbrooke church and the kitchen gardens, it faces south-east,

Cottesbrooke church beyond the old bridge, from the Park

on an axis with the distant but more attractive spire of a church three and a half miles away. The sun sparkles on the gold of the weathercock on the roof of the Hall, and on the waters of the lake.

A sharp right turn by the bootscraper at the north-eastern corner of the Middle Garden takes us through an archway and into the relatively new third enclosure or frame yard. This is a gravelled half-acre yard containing the hothouses, frames and outbuildings which were installed by greenhouse builders Messenger and Co. for the Brasseys just before the First World War. They have been so well maintained that even now, seventy years later, they are still in working order; the woodwork is freshly painted white, the glass is intact, the levers, grills and hinges are well oiled and free of rust. Great iron pipes snake above ground and below, to and fro, from house to house, filled with water pumped from two fine oil-fired boilers which operate from early September to mid-June.

This is how the auction catalogue of 1935 listed these build-ings: '*Glasshouses:* 2 peach houses, 2 vineries, 1 two-division melon and cucumber house, 1 carnation house, a plant house, 1 stove house, 2 heated plant pits, a range of heated frames. *Buildings:* fruit room, office, vegetable shed, mushroom house, stoke hole, two Robin Hood boilers, potting shed, store shed, potato store.' Doug attempts to explain the complicated system of work and heating which keeps this range of buildings, and hence the rest of the gardens, at the peak of production and beauty all round the year, but I suspect that it will take many more visits before I fully understand it. It is clear that this is the nerve centre of the gardens. This is the area that absorbs most of the work of his six kitchen garden or 'inside' gardeners. (Another five gardeners work 'out-side' in the pleasure gardens surrounding the house.)

Before Captain Brassey's glasshouses were built, the kitchen gardens were obviously run on a more modest scale, though it appears that both the frame yard and the almshouse garden were also under cultivation. By the end of the Langham era, in 1911, when funds had presumably been running low for some time, only the Middle Garden, with one greenhouse in it, was used by the Hall, though the fact that there are doors in the west walls of both the Top and the Middle Gardens suggests that both gardens had at some time been leased to the Grange. (This sombre late-Victorian building stands on the site of the old Tudor manor house.) The Top Garden was certainly leased to the Grange from 1911 until 1935 and was not used again by the Hall until then, when the estate was bought by the present family. By this time the garden had in it a large pond (enlarged from a smaller, eighteenth-century pool) surrounded by a yew hedge. Both hedge and pond have

Doug making the potato clamp

disappeared, the pond having been filled in sometime in the 1950s. It was on the site of what is now Doug's private garden. He says swallows still swoop over that area in the springtime, looking for the mud with which they, or rather their ancestors, once made their nests.

A hint of how these gardens may have been laid out at one time is provided by the height of the ground in the Top Garden. Along the western and southern walls it is considerably higher than the road outside. (The south-western corner is actually the highest point of the whole complex.) One can see quite easily over the tops of these two walls from within the garden, but outside there is a drop of at least ten feet. This strongly suggests that the Top Garden had raised walks along these two walls, if not along all of its walls, which would be typical of a Tudor garden. Little bulges on the south-east and north-east corners of the garden walls in the map of 1628 suggest that there were gazebos here too.

This introductory tour by Doug has brought us back to his house. It is now lunch time. At one o'clock Doug gave his gardeners, whom we have scarcely met, the order to down tools. Joy has already left her bench in the potting shed and gone home to make Doug and us some sandwiches. Elsewhere, in the twelve acres of pleasure gardens surrounding the Hall, the five outside gardeners are also knocking off for lunch. The pleasure gardens include lawns, shrubberies, a wild garden, a water garden, court-yards, ornamental pools and herbaceous beds. However, as my interest lies mainly in the kitchen gardens this diary will only record the work in this department. The kitchen gardens are, of course, only half of Doug's responsibility as head gardener. He is obliged to oversee all the gardens and all his eleven gardeners, both 'inside' and 'outside'.

At this point it might be useful to explain the gardeners' hierarchy. It operates at Cottesbrooke in the 1980s in much the same way as garden hierarchies always have done. In 1830, for example, John Claudius Loudon wrote in his *Encyclopaedia of Gardening*, 'The gardener who occupies a first rate situation has under him a forester, for the demesne-woods and park-trees; a pleasure-ground foreman for the lawns and shrubbery; a flower garden foreman, a forcing-department foreman, and a kitchen garden foreman.' The same applies, more or less, here at Cottes-brooke. Doug, the head gardener, works closely with the head forester and has two foremen under him in the gardens; one for 'inside' and one for 'outside', Ken being the inside foreman. (The only difference between 1984 and 1830 is that these foremen are now called chargehands.) Ken, as the most experienced gardener

Grapes and sacks of potatoes in the fruit room

after Doug, oversees 19-year-old John, his eldest son; 20-year-old Teresa, daughter of the head forester; Jess, who will work longer hours in the gardens when he retires in a year's time from his early morning postman's round; Sid, a semi-retired gardener now in his seventies who works, three half days a week, on Mondays, Tuesdays and Thursdays; and Joy who is new to gardening and only works in the mornings. John, Teresa and Jess do most of the heavy work such as digging and weeding, helped out by Sid. Joy does light work such as pricking out seedlings, potting on and tidying up pot plants. Ken and Doug, besides taking on their share of the heavy work, also have the responsibilities of fruit-tree pruning and planting, packing produce for transport to several of the family's other houses and checking and arranging the displays of pot plants in the Hall.

There are numerous other routine jobs which are shared by all the kitchen garden staff such as compost mixing, fruit, vegetable, herb and flower picking, fruit and vegetable storing, rubbish clearance, weeding and hoeing, glasshouse maintenance and repair, the watering and feeding of plants, opening and closing the glasshouse ventilators, the spraying of insecticides and fungicides, sowing outdoor seed, planting and thinning seedlings, fixing supports and protective netting. However, the orders for when, where and how all this is done come only from Doug. He is also responsible for appointments, sick leave, sackings or dismissals, the arrangement of holidays, overtime and weekend duties, and the ordering of supplies such as seeds, bulbs, fertilisers, chemicals, flower pots, tools, machinery, gloves, string and boiler fuel. Also, at various seasons and after discussion with the garden's owner (her ladyship), Doug decides on the species and varieties of species of fruit, vegetable, flower or pot plant to be grown for the house and on the planning and planting of the outside flowerbeds, courtyards and pleasure gardens. He writes all the plant labels in a clear, neat hand and sows all the seeds that have to be raised under glass. Holidays are not mentioned by Loudon, as they scarcely existed in 1830, but everyone here has ten working days off in winter and ten in summer. Sixty or seventy years ago the only holidays a gardener had were the true 'holy days' – Good Friday, Whitsun and Christmas Day.

The five outside gardeners rarely set foot in the kitchen gardens; their jobs consist mostly of topiary and hedge clipping, ornamental tree maintenance, lawn mowing and the care of the bedding displays and

fungicides & sprays

*red cabbages, the centres ruby red,
outer leaves a grey-blue, red veins*

herbaceous borders. Their responsibilities also extend to the churchyard and the lodge gardens. However, all their bedding plants are raised and hardened off in the kitchen gardens and tender outdoor perennials such as fuschias are all over-wintered in the greenhouses. These greenhouses also supply the house with all the necessary flowering pot plants, forced flowering bulbs, orchids and winter cut flowers.

The quantity of produce from three acres of kitchen garden and one of orchard is, as might be expected, immense. Besides the brassicas which are cropping now – cabbage, cauliflower and sprouts – there are also all kinds of roots – swedes, turnips, carrots, beetroots, parsnips and celeriac. The celery, newly earthed-up in its trenches, has been planted in such vast numbers that its strong scent wafts up whenever the wind ruffles its leaves. There is a bed of leeks some 40 feet long and 10 feet wide, with leeks in it as thick as a baby's arm. Doug tells me that leeks have been grown in this same border for sixteen years. In the polythene tunnel there are French beans which have been bearing since July, also tomatoes, lettuces, salad onions, aubergines, chilli peppers, capsicums and cucumbers. As it is warm and dry in the poly tunnel it is also being used as a temporary store for several bales of straw, just delivered from the Home Farm for the potato clamp, which is a temporary, outdoor arrangement for storing potatoes. Here too are barrow-loads of the potatoes which will be put in the clamp. There is also a heap of bulb onions, dried off and ready to be sorted and stored in one of the old out-houses.

The fruit store is a cool, dark, windowless but well-ventilated room with slatted wooden shelves on either side of a narrow gangway. The shelves are almost filled with early and mid-season apples and pears. Large vegetable marrows have one section to themselves and bunches of black and white grapes hang against the end wall on strings. The old gardening books describe many different ways of keeping grapes, from hanging them in a dry, airy room with apples or turnips stuck to their stems, to packing them in airtight casks of bran. Or, by skilful management of the temperature and ventilation of a vinery, late-maturing varieties could be left on the vine until well into the winter. The fashion for grape bottles appears to have originated in France in the 1870s and their suitability for the task of preserving whole bunches was often discussed in the gardening journals of the day. The Fruit Growers' Guide reported that grapes of the 'Lady Downes' variety had been kept in bottles at Floors Castle (in Roxburghshire) till June 10. There were storage racks there for literally hundreds of grape bottles. The grapes were left on the vine until Christmas and were then transferred to bottles. The bottles (which were burgundy-shaped) were filled with plain, soft water. This was kept pure by a piece of charcoal. Enough wood was cut with each bunch to reach the bottom of the bottle. The *Journal of Horticulture* of 1872 reported that 'at Heaton Grange, Bolton, the gardener [John Potts] cut his last bottled grape on May 12 and the first new grapes the same day.'

Doug has planted some late-keeping varieties of grape to extend the season, and may well use the bottles to keep them when they produce enough bunches. At the moment, however, none of the grapes grown here is the right kind for that storage method but he demonstrates it to us with a few bunches, so that Hugh can take a photograph. We also note a few late plums, strawberries, raspberries and figs in plastic punnets, ready for sending to the kitchens of the big house. With this delivery Doug will also be sending a selection of the brassicas and roots that are now cropping and some of the produce from the polythene tunnel. Nothing that a greengrocer's or florist's might sell, except for oranges or lemons, is ever bought. Much of what is sent to the house is accounted for by the staff which is, by today's standards, unusually large. At weekends too (especially in the shooting season), the house might be filled with family or at least twelve guests. This means that Thursdays and Fridays are usually the busiest days for the gardeners. Doug receives his order for the kitchen from the butler, who has already discussed the menu with the cook, and her ladyship.

Everything has to be fresh for the weekends. There have to be enough cut flowers, whatever the season, to fill up to half a dozen vases in the downstairs rooms plus a few for upstairs. The jardinières and planters in the downstairs rooms, on the staircase and in the hall account for never less than sixty pot plants a week, and these are changed on Thursdays or Fridays too.

Until I saw the kitchen gardens and hothouses at Cottesbrooke I had not previously understood the extent to which such places were used. A great deal of work goes into the production of fruit and vegetables, but the raising of all the flowers and pot plants for the house takes place here as well.

In order to keep up this supply the gardeners here have to play a constant game of chess with their pot plants and seed trays. Thanks to the carefully related ratio beween the space to be heated and the diameter of the pipes heating it, each greenhouse has a different, but constant, temperature. This means that plants that are coming on too fast can be moved to a cooler house, while those that need a bit of encouragement will be moved to a warmer one. At the moment the cut flowers are: outdoor chrysanthemums and gladioli, perpetual flowering carnations and geraniums. The pot plants available for display are: *Begonia eliator* and *Begonia caribbean*, gloxinias, fuchsias, cyclamen, browallia, pot chrysanthemums and, for greenery, lemon-scented geraniums and asparagus fern.

It seems a little odd that none of the wonderful dahlias in the bed by Doug's house is being cut for the house but apparently everything has its appropriate time; the time for dahlias is not now but only from when they start flowering in mid-July till when her ladyship goes to Scotland in mid-August. Thus, although they are in flower for almost four months, they are only sent to the house for the first of those months. Her ladyship returns from Scotland in late September; from then on the gardeners will send chrysanthemums.

*cyclamen
(pale pink flowers)*

There are other traditions; garden produce is sent all over the country from time to time, to other members of the family and Doug keeps a careful note of everything that goes on in the gardens, every day, in his Gardens Journal. Next week, he says, they will start clamping the potatoes; he will send for us to record this event as soon as they do so. After we left he wrote, 'Visited by Sue Campbell and Hugh Palmer, for the purpose of writing about kitchen gardens.'

Second visit Monday, 22 October 1984

It is a filthy day, warm but very wet. Doug has telephoned to say that they have begun building the potato clamp. They actually started it a week ago, choosing a corner in the Middle Garden beside the new bungalow and waiting until there had been enough rain to dampen the ground; it's no good, apparently, making a potato clamp on dry ground, as the potatoes need a bit of moisture for keeping by this method. This is the first year Doug has made an old-fashioned potato clamp at Cottesbrooke. The year before, in his first winter here, the potatoes were stored as usual in bins in the sheds behind the old greenhouses. By March they had started sprouting, and worse, rotting. Doug is confident that his clamp will avoid those troubles and last well into the spring.

The first potatoes to be clamped are the early main crops, 'Romano' and 'Drayton'. 'Pentland Ivory', 'Wilja' and 'Estima' have also been lifted from the Middle Garden and these will be the first to be used. The potatoes stand in a huge, flat-topped, barrow-shaped mound covered with a neat coat of earth a foot thick. The end on which work is to be continued is temporarily covered with sacks. As Ken pulls them away we can see that the potatoes are lying on a thick bed of yellow straw, with another thick layer of straw between them and their overcoat of earth. The clamp extends lengthways with each new load of potatoes. The potatoes for a clamp need to be large and roughly all the same size. This is to keep the air moving round them while they are in the clamp, and to stop them sweating, which would lead to rot. Small potatoes mixed with large ones would obstruct the air-flow. Barrow-loads of unsuitable potatoes have already been sorted out and carted away for the pigs, or to anyone who wants them. I am dazed by the quantities; there must be 50 hundredweight of potatoes in this crop alone, and there are still the 'Majestic' and 'Desirées' to come – the later longer-keeping potatoes which have yet to be dug in the Top Garden.

The clamp has been marked out in a strip six feet wide. Ken and Teresa cover the strip with a bed of straw nine inches thick and heap the potatoes in the middle, leaving a foot of straw uncovered at each side. The heap tapers in as it rises. When it is about two and a half feet high they flatten the top and cover this and the sides with another nine-inch-thick layer of straw. At five feet intervals an upright bundle of straw is stuffed into the top, at the centre. These bundles act as ventilators for the steam and warm air that will be generated by the clamped potatoes. Lastly comes the thick, smooth coat of earth; as it is dug a trench is formed all along the sides of the clamp. When it rains the trench will act as a drain for the water that runs down the sides of the clamp. If the winter gets very cold, more earth can be heaped over it by widening the trench. This first earth overcoat is just patted down, leaving the top four

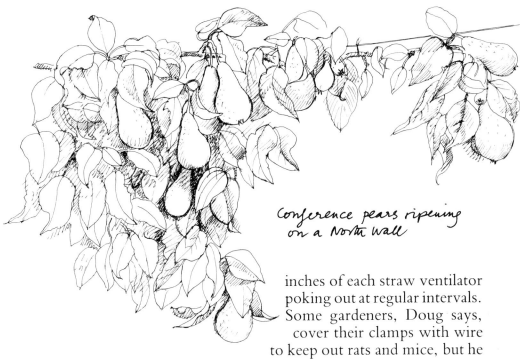

Conference pears ripening on a North Wall

inches of each straw ventilator poking out at regular intervals. Some gardeners, Doug says, cover their clamps with wire to keep out rats and mice, but he puts his faith in Rodney, his elegant, coal-black garden cat.

Although it is only a fortnight since our first visit, there are several noticeable changes in the gardens. The dahlias are still in full bloom, but they have been spoiled by the recent bad weather. The last of the grapes (the 'Buckland Sweetwater') have been picked and carefully examined by Ken for rotten fruit before being hung in the fruit room, which is now full; the last of the orchard's apples and pears were picked on Friday with seven hundredweight of fruit ('Lord Derby') from two of the apple trees alone. Potatoes for immediate use are waiting, washed and packed in sacks.

Mention of the Lord Derby apple in connection with the fruit room reminds me of an account of Lord Derby's own fruit rooms at Knowsley near Liverpool. It illustrates how much Lord Derby liked his fruit and how important the fruit room could be. The writer is James Anderson, in his *New Practical Gardener* of *c*1880. 'One of the most commodious and one of the best fruit-rooms that we have seen, is in the gardens of the Earl of Derby ... There is capacity for storing an immense number of kinds of fruits, and breadth of walking space for any one to inspect them. The late Lord Derby seemed to prefer to have a look in the fruit-room, after the same fashion as he liked to walk into the houses and see the fruit growing; and quite right. It is a most interesting sight to see a variety of fruits nicely arranged in preserving order in a good house. It is too often the case that fruit-rooms are narrow, and not suited to the wants of a place. Why not have them as stylish in their way as plant-rooms or fruit-growing rooms or houses, as they are generally called?'

The polythene tunnel has been cleared of all its tomatoes, chillis, capsicums, cucumbers and aubergines; the ground made clear by their removal has already been dug over and made ready for plantings of early peas, broad beans, winter salads, early cabbages and cauliflowers. Ugly though it may be, the poly tunnel is one of Doug's proudest introductions to the gardens. He needed somewhere to bring on early produce, and whereas a new greenhouse of this size would have cost £4,500, the tunnel cost just one-tenth of that sum. He says it can be moved and re-erected in half a day and although it costs nothing to heat, any crop grown in it will be in advance of an outdoor crop by up to six weeks. Even though the polythene will disintegrate in two and a half years, it costs only £70 to re-cover, and if it tears it can be mended with tape. Last summer and spring this tunnel, besides producing all the crops that have just been removed, was used for growing 'Ogen' melons to follow on from hothouse melons, potatoes that were ready to eat by the end of April and strawberries that were ripe in mid-May. It also supplied the house with a continual crop of salads all through winter. The desire to have luxuries out of season goes back in garden history to at least as far as the Romans and it is rather satisfying to see that here at Cottesbrooke the tradition is being kept alive by Doug. I swallow my aversion to the poly tunnel's appearance by having to admit that it serves its purpose very well.

The hazelnuts, cob nuts and filberts, have also been picked. They were dried off first in the boiler room, then patiently de-husked by Joy and put in boxes, to be stored in the fruit room till Christmas. There will also be new potatoes for Christmas, 'just for the dining room' (which is Doug's way of saying not for the whole house). These are being grown at the moment in very large pots in the coolest part of the vinery and are already quite leafy. They were planted on Midsummer's Day and left outdoors till the cold weather began. Doug is particularly proud of his potatoes; he grows several varieties including the violet-skinned 'Edzell Blues' and the delicious sausage-shaped 'Pink Fir Apple'. For size and yield though, he likes 'Drayton'; although the crop was badly affected this year by slugs he had one record potato weighing two and a half pounds, and two of his lifted plants (which he calls 'shows') yielded 14½ pounds of potatoes between them.

cob nuts

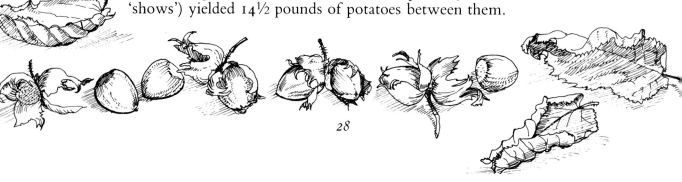

28

Ken trimming grapes in the wash room

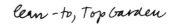

lean-to, Top Garden

The three-quarter span vinery where the potatoes are being forced is the largest of all the hothouses. It stands, as is usual, against the south-facing wall of the greenhouse yard and is divided into two sections, each 30 feet long and 18 feet wide. A bright-red geranium, vigorously flowering, is trained up the back wall; the vines, as is also usual, are planted at the front of the house and are then trained in single rods to grow high up under the roof. These vines actually have their roots inside the house; the traditional method of growing them so that their roots occupy an outside border has been dropped, and the holes through which the rods would have entered the house are blocked. Doug's explanation for this break with tradition is that modern gardeners use modern fertilisers. There is therefore no longer any need to feed their vines from outside with rich manure and the odd bits of carrion, such as dead sheep, pigs, dogs or cats, which as he puts it 'tend to pong a bit in the summer'. The hot water pipes are above the ground here ('to heat the air, not the soil'), giving the vinery a temperature of 45° to 55° Fahrenheit. A peach house 30 feet long is attached to each side of the vinery, thus creating one building 120 feet long. However, as the peach houses are only 14 feet wide, the temperature here is more like 55°F.

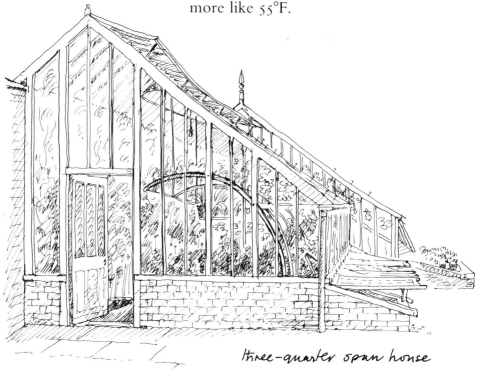

three-quarter span house

Perhaps I should explain here exactly what gardeners mean when they refer to 'lean-to', 'span' and 'three-quarter span' houses or frames. A lean-to house is so called because the structure literally leans against a tall back wall; usually a lean-to house is south-facing. The earliest nineteenth-century hothouses were all lean-tos, built exactly like glazed sheds. The boiler heating the lean-to was either attached to the side of the hothouse or given a shed of its own on the northern back-side of the wall. Other buildings, or back-sheds as they were called, such as bothies for the gardeners, mushroom houses, potting sheds and fruit stores were also to be found on this side of the wall. The two old greenhouses on the wall between the Top and Middle Gardens were arranged like this. The remains of boiler houses, a bothy and storage sheds are still to be seen there. The frame yard of 1911 was laid out in a more practical manner however, with the boiler house, potting shed and so on on the eastern wall and the fruit house, wash room and office on the western wall.

A span house is a free-standing building with a glazed, ridged roof and glazed walls all round. The heat is brought to it by means of underground pipes. A three-quarter span house has literally three-quarters of the amount of roof of a span house, with a moderately high wall forming the northern side. If the roof of a span house is seen to have two halves, meeting at the ridge, the term 'three-quarter span' is self-explanatory. The ridge of the roof of a three-quarter span house is higher than the back wall, giving the plants inside it (usually vines or peaches) the advantage of extra growing space, as well as some northern light.

I am beginning to understand how the design of a greenhouse is dictated by the use for which it is intended. Doug points out that the pathways have iron grilles so that plants can be watered and fed through them. The grilles are decorative but also functional. They stand on invisible underground pillars to allow freedom for the roots. According to Charles MacIntosh, writing in 1828 in his *Practical Gardener*, the footpaths in greenhouses were originally 'mere planks, laid upon the borders to walk on'. Or they could have been made of 'lattice-work ... supported on blocks of wood in order to admit the sun and air to the border below, and to prevent its being much trodden on by walking'. But already gardeners had found that 'the neatest and most permanent [paths] are constructed of cast-iron plates, made to rest upon props, at a proper

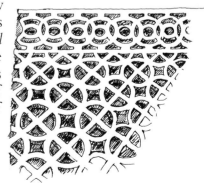

Messenger's floor-grating

height from the ground. These cast-iron gratings can be made to any pattern and of lengths convenient for their being removed . . . These gratings are well adapted where the path passes along above the flue, as they not only prevent the covers from being broken, but also allow the free escape of heat.'

The borders of these houses slope towards the paths so that they drain into them. The wired metal trellises curving from front to back of each peach house are made no higher than a man's reach so that a gardener can tend the trees and pick the fruit comfortably, while the length of the branches and therefore the yield is increased within a very small space. By training the trees against these curved trellises the sloping roof of the house is kept clear, allowing sun and light to reach the trees trained up against the back wall. The peach houses are used for nectarines as well as peaches and one of the trellises is actually occupied by a fig tree; unorthodox, as figs should really have a house to themselves. Another, even less orthodox use of the peach houses and the vinery is to fill their beds from end to end with pots of enormous, shaggy-mop-flowered chrysanthemums of every hue. They have just been brought in from the yard outside so that they can continue to flower. There is no space for them in any of the other houses, and it is one of the unalterable customs at Cottesbrooke that chrysanthemums are to be cut for the house from late September until Christmas.

On this visit, Doug lets me take notes from the journal in his office. He records the weather; I see that on October 18 he had 'strong winds and rain, but the glasshouses were OK thanks to having the foresight to get Jess to re-fasten all the panes with copper nails during the past few weeks.' The wind also 'blew down the bean poles and knocked the dahlias about but the rest of the garden was surprisingly intact.' He also records what's being sent to the house – the same fruit, flowers and vegetables as on our last visit, with the exception of the figs, plums and soft fruit (now over) and the gloxinias and fuchsias; what's been mended (one of the Hall gardens' lawnmowers and those various panes of glass in the cold frames and hot-houses); what's been ordered from outside (flower pots, spring bulbs from Parker's and bales of straw

Red Beauty chrysanthemum

from the Home Farm for the potato clamp); who's been off sick; who's on weekend duty; what's been sown, pricked out, potted or planted – lettuce, forcing antirrhinum, schizanthus, broad beans, early peas (sown and later pricked out); regal pelargoniums, zonal pelargonium cuttings, carnation cuttings, freesia corms, standard geraniums, cinerarias, amaryllis bulbs and calceolaria (potted on or potted up); what's been sprayed, drenched or smoked against what and with what, et cetera. 'Potting on' is the term used when a plant is taken from a small pot and put into a larger one, but when seedlings are transferred from trays to their first pot the correct term is 'potted up'.

Doug's office is in a corner of the greenhouse yard. From the window over his desk he can see all the comings and goings of his gardeners. He has an ingenious arrangement for storing his packets of seed. It consists of three wooden fruit trays stacked on top of one another. Each is divided into four compartments, each compartment is labelled for a different month and the seeds to be sown in that particular month are slotted neatly in it. As the year progresses the box on top is placed underneath. At the moment the box labelled Sept., Oct., Nov. and Dec. is on top. Doug also uses two seed trays for his correspondence. One is labelled 'In' and the other 'Soddit'. Also in his office: a rabbit's tail, the annual gift of the head game keeper. This is a fresh tail. As soon as it is quite dry and mummified, which will be in four to six weeks, it

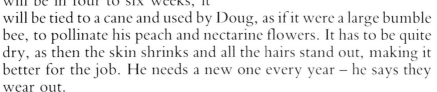

trug full of autumn veg.

will be tied to a cane and used by Doug, as if it were a large bumble bee, to pollinate his peach and nectarine flowers. It has to be quite dry, as then the skin shrinks and all the hairs stand out, making it better for the job. He needs a new one every year – he says they wear out.

The next event of any note at Cottesbrooke will be the wedding of her ladyship's grand-daughter on November 3. Besides supplying the flowers for the house the gardeners will have to supplement the flower arrangements for the church with bamboo, ivy, box, mahonia, berberis and coloured leaves from the park and pleasure gardens. The gardeners must also put new, finer gravel on the churchyard paths. At present it is too coarse for the ladies to walk on in high heels.

rabbit's tail pollinator

NOVEMBER

Third visit Wednesday, 21 November 1984

The weather has been typical of November; to quote various entries from Doug's journal it's been 'miserable', 'cold', 'wet', 'dull' and 'foggy'. Today is beautiful and as soon as we arrive Doug takes us round the gardens to see what's happened in the month since our last visit.

The potato clamp has been completed; the last two varieties to be put in it were 'Desirée' and 'Cara'. It is now about 30 feet long and lies in its sheltered corner with five bright little yellow straw ventilators poking out of the dark chocolate-coloured earth with which it is covered. There is one snag: a rat has got in. The gardeners know this because they found his hole at the top. They have filled it in, and if it's disturbed again they'll know he's still there and they'll take the whole thing to pieces until they find him. I ask Doug what they'll do then and he says the whole workforce will be waiting with spades to bat him as he runs out. Doug is pretty fed up with his cat Rodney. Apart from the rat in the potato clamp there was one (now killed) in one of the old store rooms and, as the journal for November 6 notes, 'We have mice present in the top span frame. Traps have been placed in it.' One mouse was caught on the 7th and two on the 8th. (The traps were baited with hazelnuts which proved 'very effective'.)

The flower borders in all three gardens, Top, Middle and frame yard, are completely empty – all the dahlias, chrysanthemums and gladioli have been cut down, and dug up. Their supporting canes have been bundled up and put to dry in the boiler house. Tubers and corms have had their stems cut off. They have been drenched with a fungicide so that they can be stored in boxes under the bench in the potting shed. The runner bean poles have also been bundled up and stored in the box shed next to the potting shed.

In the vinery and peach houses fallen leaves have had to be cleared up every day.

hazelnut bait

Tank for washing pots in the mushroom house

The vine rods are now quite bare. Yesterday Ken was able to start pruning them ('back to three eyes', according to Doug's journal). As there are five main hothouses, the four full-time gardeners and Doug have one hothouse each as their own special responsibility. John minds the stove house, Jess the carnation house, Teresa the palm house and Doug the propagation house. The vinery range is Ken's house. Tomorrow he will start untying the peaches from their supports, prune them, spray them and the walls behind them and then tie them up again. He can only do this where the ground is clear enough for the branches to fall right forward, so all the pot plants will have to be moved out of the way. As soon as the chrysanthemums in the vinery have finished flowering he will lower the pruned vine rods, clean off their peeling bark and spray them too.

Work is now definitely decreasing outdoors and increasing indoors. The gardens are cleared of root crops and old brassica stumps. The last potatoes, carrots and beetroots have been dug up; the grass in the orchard has had its last mowing; the fruit cage netting is still in place but it has been carefully mended.

As soon as it becomes dry enough the cleared ground will be manured and dug over, but when the weather drives the gardeners indoors there is no lack of work – there are composts to mix, rotten fruit to be picked out of the fruit in store and flower pots to wash.

primulas – obconica and kewensis

Doug has checked over his supplies of pesticides and fertilisers, gone through his catalogues and ordered his next batches of seed.

The free-standing span greenhouses are stuffed with pot plants which are either in full flower or about to flower, so that in a month's time, by Christmas, there will be plenty of forced bulbs, carnations, geraniums, orchids, cinerarias, cyclamen, primulas (*obconica* and *kewensis*), begonias and calceolarias for the house. Looking even further ahead, to spring, Doug will have clivias, daffodils, narcissi, antirrhinums and stocks for cutting. He is very proud of his pot plants at the moment. Where they have been massed together in Teresa's house (nicknamed 'the palm house' because just one tall palm grows in a pot in the middle) they absolutely sparkle with colour and freshness. The sky shows clear blue through the glass and the late November sun is very bright.

Apart from the winter pruning and digging there is one outdoor job of some importance which remains to be done; this is the making of a carrot clamp. There are three enormous heaps of carrots in the poly tunnel, all recently dug up. One heap is the variety 'Flacoro', one is 'Vita Longa' and one is 'Oranza'. (I do begin to wonder how modern nurserymen think up these names.) Ken and Teresa keep each variety separate, but sort them into large and small, and cut off the tops. The carrot clamp is to go next to the potato clamp and, like the potato clamp, it will be insulated with straw and earth. Because of the shape of a carrot, the carrot clamp will be dome-shaped, rather than barrow-shaped. Ken says he hasn't made one for fifteen years; like the potatoes, the carrots always used to be stored here in a shed, and most went rotten before winter was out.

To make the carrot clamp a circle eight feet across is marked out on clean ground. A thick bed of straw is laid on it, then the largest carrots are laid in a ring, points inwards, with a foot-wide margin of straw all round. The longest keepers ('Flacoro') are the first to be laid down. When the clamp is finished it should look like an upturned pudding basin, so each ring of carrots has to be slightly smaller than its predecessor. When the circle of large carrots is high enough to form a little wall the smaller carrots are flung, higgledy-piggledy, into the centre. Ken levels up the top of the wall by carefully inserting small carrots crossways between the pointed ends of the large carrots. When the 'Flacoros' are finished Teresa arranges a thin layer of straw over them to separate them from the next batch which will be 'Vita Longa'. Ken works carefully and patiently, telling Teresa what to do. She, never having made a carrot clamp before, appears to be enjoying the task, stepping back from time to time like a child making a sandcastle and admiring the ingenuity of it. As she goes off for another barrow-load of carrots Ken gently neatens up the side of the dome, which is now nearly knee-high, but not as circular as he would like it. When it is finished the clamp will be about three and a half feet high, with a straw ventilator in the top, then a thick undercoat of straw, then an overcoat of earth and a trench all round it. There will be six to eight hundredweight of carrots in it in all, without the 'Oranzas', which are to be stored in a shed and used first.

Before we leave I ask Doug to give me the pattern of his day. It goes like this: he gets up around 6.30 am, has a cup of Teasmade tea and goes up to the Hall with Ken at seven o'clock. They check all the floral arrangements and pots, changing plants if necessary, watering them and replacing cut flowers in vases if necessary. (This week besides the usual chrysanthemums and carnations they will have strelizias, agapanthus and two kinds of orchids, *cypripedium* and *cymbidium*). He's back in the gardens by 8 or 8.30 am if it's a change-over day for all the indoor arrangements. They have to look good on Fridays, for the weekend guests. He then has breakfast, after which he makes his delivery of vegetables and fruit to the Hall kitchen. This weekend there's a shooting party of about twelve guests, which with the resident staff means that this Friday he will have to take:

30 lb potatoes	*8 lb carrots*	*10 lb cabbage*
2 large heads celery	*8 lb parsnips*	*6 or 8 lb sprouts*
3 or 4 celeriacs	*4 or 5 lb swede*	*kale and cauliflower*
3 lb onions	*15 to 20 large leeks*	*6 lb cooking apples*
sage, thyme, parsley,		*4 lb eating apples*
mint, chives (all fresh)		*2 lb pears*

parsley, sage and thyme

Salads (and soft fruit, when in season) are sent up every day. Other kinds of vegetables are sent every other day. Once the vegetables have been delivered work continues in the gardens, with a half-hour mid-morning coffee break and an hour from one to two o'clock for lunch. Work begins for the rest of the gardeners at 8 am (10 am for Jess) and ends at five o'clock. There are seasonal differences though. For three weeks either side of Christmas, when it becomes impossible to work outdoors because of the dark, the staff can go home at half-past four. On the other hand in the summer when the days are long and hot there is overtime to be done in the evenings; watering, closing ventilators and removing shades. There is also a weekend roster, for which one gardener (either Ken, John or one of the outside gardeners) is appointed as dutyman. He has to take care of the kitchen garden and all the hothouses for the whole of Saturday and Sunday. Every Friday afternoon before work ends Doug shows the dutyman all the plants needing special attention, then hands him a set of garden keys before locking up. On Mondays Doug walks round all his gardens, inspecting them and planning the week's work. Occasionally he accompanies her ladyship on a similar tour of inspection. Every other Monday he takes the time sheets to the Estate Office; every other Thursday he hands out the wages. On Fridays he sees that all the pot plants are fed with liquid fertiliser. Friday is also the day for changing the flowers on the family grave.

This weekly or fortnightly routine has a familiar ring to it. On getting home I look up John Evelyn's *Directions for the Gardiner at Sayes-Court*, written in 1686. (Sayes Court, near Deptford, was Evelyn's home for fifty years.) 'The Gardiner', he wrote, 'should walke aboute the whole Gardens every Monday-morning duely, not omitting the least corner, and so observe what Flowers or Trees & plants want staking, binding and redressing, watering, or in danger; especially after great stormes, & high winds and then immediately to reforme, establish, shade, water &c what he finds amisse, before he go about any other work.' ... 'Every fortnight looke on Saturday to your seede and roote boxes, to aire & preserve them from mouldinesse & vermine' ... 'The tooles are to be carried into the Toole-house, and all other instruments set in their places, every night when you leave work: & in wett weather you are to clense, sharpen and repaire them' ... 'The Gardner, is every night to aske what Rootes, sallading, garnishing, &c will be used the next day, which he is accordingly to bring to the Cook in the morning; and therefore from time to time to informe her what garden provision & fruite is ripe and in season to be spent ...'

Evelyn also has a nice description of how to prune a vine, which describes the appearance of the vine rods here exactly. 'In pruning vines', he says, 'cut so close as to resemble a ragged-staff onely not above 2 or 3 eyes or buds, upon the bearing-branches is enough, & the lower the vine, & fewer the branches, the better the Grapes'.

The day-to-day running of these gardens seems to be almost the same as it would have been, if not in

'a ragged staff'

Doug in the vinery

Evelyn's time, then certainly a hundred years
ago. Appearances, though, are quite different.
Most of the gardeners, both male and
female, wear jeans, padded nylon
anoraks or windcheaters, tweed jackets,
battered waxed-cotton Barbour coats, green or
blue boilersuits and heavy wellingtons or training shoes, depending on the weather. Doug is
neatly dressed in a tweed jacket, gaberdine
trousers and heavy outdoor shoes. He sometimes wears a flat tweed cap for warmth. He
says if he were to look like a pre-war
gardener he would have to wear a bowler
hat or a trilby, a fly-away collar with a
bow-tie (a long tie would flop forward on to
his work), a green apron and spotlessly clean
leather boots.

On getting home I also look up potato
and carrot storing. Adam the Gardener (the
Sunday Express c1930) recommends
making clamps above ground almost
exactly like Doug's, so do the late Victorians,
but earlier writers such as Bradley (*Kalendar*,
1720) preferred to dig pits or trenches, burying
roots for winter store in sand, and roofing them
with wheat straw and sometimes, but not always,
a layer of earth.

DECEMBER

Fourth visit Tuesday, 18 December 1984

Luckily we have chosen another fine day for a visit to the gardens. It is cold, frosty and bright. On our arrival we find Doug and Ken in the vinery range, pruning the fig which has been trained over the curved trellis in the top peach house. The peaches and nectarines have already been pruned, sprayed and tied back neatly to their wires; as they will be the first fruit trees to flower they have to be the first to be pruned. Their flower buds are already beginning to swell. Doug says that the fig should really have a house to itself, rather than share one with peaches, for the simple reason that its great leaves take too much light from the peaches on the wall behind. He explains it very clearly. 'Figs have shady leaves, as their fruit ripens in the shade, but peaches need sun to ripen, which is why they have narrow, light-filtering leaves.'

Nevertheless, two of his peach trees ('Peregrines') produced 600 peaches between them last year. About 200 of them happened to ripen all at once, (as is their habit, apparently) on a Saturday. You can't leave them once they ripen or they fall splat on the floor, so Doug and Joy spent the whole evening picking them.

The point of a 'Peregine' peach, Doug tells me, is that 99 per cent of it consists of delicious juice; it has white flesh, is soft-skinned and is so delicate that it can never be packed or sent away. Fortunately, the hothouse peaches ripen between June and August, before her ladyship leaves for her holidays in Scotland. 'They could never be grown commercially, they bruise so easily. You can mark them by touching them even before they ripen.' Doug remembers with horror a day in May when the gardens were open to the public and he had not thought it was neces-sary to lock the peach houses. 'A stupid woman went through the house shrieking "Peaches! Peaches!" She touched some of them and, even though they were still green when she did it, when they

secateurs and string, for pruning

Primula obconica and cyclamen in the Palm House

ripened every one that she'd handled had a huge bruise on it.' I am reminded of the traditional dislike that gardeners have for women (other than weeding women) in their gardens and their anxiety about any house with precious fruit in it.

The pruning of the fig is executed by Ken, with Doug advising. Between them they are transforming the thick crowded tangle of last year's branches and side shoots into an orderly, spreading, hand-shaped arrangement, with long, thin, tapering fingers curving neatly over the trellis. All the old wood, the greyest branches, is being cut out, leaving the younger, darker, greener growth to bear fruit next year. Ken also removes the smallest twigs, leaving nothing that is thinner than one of his fingers. None of this operation looks like any of the diagrams in books that I have tried to use when pruning my own figs. Doug and Ken laugh at the idea that anything as variable as a fig tree could be made into such a thing as a diagram. Their job is not made any easier by the inflexibility of some of the older branches and they occasionally snap, no matter how careful Ken is. The tree is being coaxed by degrees into a proper shape, after years of neglect. After pruning Ken sprays it, and brushes off the woolly aphids with a concoction smelling strongly of disinfectant. He then ties the branches in again, leaving the winter-fruit on the branches. It will either grow on and form the first crop in late June, or drop off of its own accord. Ken is a tall man in his mid-fifties; John is the eldest of his four children. A trace of a Lancashire accent gives the clue to where he was born and brought up. He started his working life as a butcher's boy, which in war-time was not a very satisfying job. He then turned to gardening, and stayed with it. He works calmly and slowly, stopping work completely when he is spoken to.

As the vinery borders outside are not now planted with the actual roots of the vines, winter lettuces and cauliflowers are growing here instead. They do well here as they have two advantages: they face due south and a little warmth is reflected from the glass of the vinery behind.

In the wash room next to the fruit store John and Teresa are busy trimming and scrubbing leeks, onions, swedes, parsnips and beetroots.

young cauliflower

Teresa stands at the large shallow stone sink (it is almost six feet long), brushing the roots in a bowl of cold water; her fingernails have been varnished, presumably for an outing at the weekend. They are all chipped now with the rough work she has to do. This is the room to which all the produce is brought before it is despatched to the house. The sink stands under a window with stone draining boards on either side. It is furnished with one cold tap, one or two scrubbing brushes and a few plastic bowls of various sizes. A hefty pair of scales stands on the right-hand draining board. Various tools and sieves hang on the walls and long tresses of raffia are tied in a bundle on the back of the fruit-room door. Buckets and green tin vases of the kind used by florists occupy a corner of the left-hand draining board. Behind Teresa, John is trimming the roots and tops from the leeks which he has dug and brought here in a wheelbarrow. Against the back wall there is a low work bench with shelves above; these are stacked with wooden and cardboard boxes, green plastic trugs and folded sacks. Below the bench there are coiled hosepipes and wood-wool for packing. The leeks are now neat and almost clean enough to be cooked straightaway; they are laid tidily in a box, green at one end and white at the other. Next the onions are fetched from the shed where they are stored; their withered stems and loose skins are neatly removed. John wears spectacles and works close to his work, mostly in silence. Although there is still a week to go before Christmas the root vegetables are being prepared now. Yesterday the order went out to start collecting holly for the Hall and the church as the birds have begun to eat the berries. It is her ladyship's ninetieth birthday on Christmas Eve which makes it a somewhat special occasion; including servants there will be thirty or forty people in the house. John and Teresa are also to start cutting cabbages today, both Savoys and reds. Out in the garden it is so cold, and the cabbages are so large, that discs of ice the size of dinner plates have formed in the cabbages' lower leaves.

For the décor over Christmas there will be chrysanthemums, orchids, nerines, geraniums, freesias and carnations as cut flowers. Pot plants will include forced hyacinths and narcissi, begonias, cyclamen and cinerarias. This is the cook's order. It will have to last from Christmas till January 3 as Christmas Day is a Tuesday, but there is plenty of last summer's produce in the freezer to supplement this delivery:

20 lb of sprouts	*new potatoes*	*20 swedes*	*fresh herbs*
10 Savoy cabbages	*(from the tubs*	*5 lb beetroot*	*20 parsnips*
4 red cabbages	*in the vinery)*	*apples* } *from fruit store*	*2 trugs of kale*
about 20 onions	*1 cwt old potatoes*	*pears*	

Celery is noticeably absent from the list; unfortunately it has been badly attacked by slugs.

Digging has started in the gardens, some parts are being manured – others not. The wall pears in the Top Garden have been pruned, and pruning has begun in the orchards. In fact, digging and pruning have been the main activities this month. Doug waited for a sunny but frosty day before pruning the wall fruit; 'You need sun so that your fingers don't get too cold, and frost so that the borders are firm enough to be stood on without needing digging again.' The carrot clamp was finished right at the beginning of the month and the rat was caught by poison – Ken saw its tail disappearing into the carrot clamp before it was finished, but there are still 'legions of mice' needing to be trapped according to Doug's journal.

The poly tunnel has been rotavated and planted with broad beans, peas, strawberries, lettuce, cauliflowers, parsley and radishes. Space has been left for salad onions, bunching carrots and early potatoes. Inside this tunnel spring seems to have begun already. Its warm, sheltered envelope of air makes quite a contrast with the cold, tightly clenched atmosphere outside.

In the frame yard the glass of the span frames has been scrubbed, inside and out, with a special cleanser and where it is broken Jess has replaced it. Like the digging and pruning this is a job that will continue for a few more weeks after Christmas, though as far as outdoor work is concerned there is little else to do here except mend, clean and clear. Only in Doug's office is there any hint of the busy months ahead. His sweet pea seeds have arrived (a collection of eight varieties, with romantic names like 'Old Times', 'Hunter's Moon', 'Ballerina' and 'Eclipse'). Seven varieties of primula, the seeds of seventeen varieties of other herbaceous plants ranging alphabetically from astilbes to *Zelkova serrata* and thirty-four packets of vegetable seed have also arrived, along with lily bulbs, winter wash, putty, some new rakes, slime remover and sulphur candles.

We leave at 3.30pm. It is very cold and dark but everything in the gardens has been made bright, clean and tidy; both gardens and gardeners seem to be waiting for the turning point of the year.

Ken pruning and tying the fig

J A N U A R Y

We were not to know it, but because of bad weather and our own winter holidays it was mid-February, two months, before we were to see the gardens again. Everything that is written in this diary for January is therefore taken from Doug's journal, and from what we saw of the gardens when January came round again in 1986.

Doug installed four new thermometers, three in the greenhouses and one outside his office about the middle of the month; his journal records the temperature in centigrade for the first two weeks and Fahrenheit thereafter. Either way the thermometers registered what was all too plain – it was extremely cold. The temperature rarely rose above freezing outdoors throughout the month and often stood well below. In the early morning of January 17 it dipped to an amazing 6°F or −14°C.

'It was so cold', wrote Doug, 'that the glass on the stove and palm houses froze over.' Both these houses were designed to maintain temperatures of 60° to 75°F and 55° to 65°F respectively. The temperature in the lean-to greenhouse in the Top Garden (heated by Calor gas) slipped to 40°F and in the fig house it fell to 32°F. 'Frost got in', Doug recorded dolefully. Luckily no irreversible damage was done, except to the freesias and cinerarias lodged there. It also began to snow early in the month. With the first sprinkling of that, all the gardeners were bidden to help remove the net from the top of the fruit cage, in case it broke under the weight of a heavy fall which came, sure enough, later on in the middle of the month. (The fruit cage measures 90 by 60 feet and the top net is actually 95 by 65 feet in size.) To protect the plants in unheated frames, rugs, old carpets, sacks and blankets were laid over the lights. If the weather was fine enough in the mornings they were rolled back to let in light and

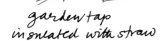

garden tap insulated with straw

Chicory and its forcing pot

warmth. By the 28th, however, the weather was 'so fine, mild and sunny that the houses needed ventilating from mid-morning onwards.' The snow had gone but there was still frost in the ground. The potato clamp was given a thicker overcoat of earth and Doug half-filled a few more large plastic tubs with seed potatoes and put them in the vinery for early forcing. He will top them up as the shoots grow.

With such hard weather there was little work to be done outside except pruning. All the free-standing outdoor trees had been pruned between Christmas and January 18, but after that the bitter cold kept the workforce indoors for ten days. Then, when warmer weather returned, Doug, Ken and young John began pruning and tying in the wall fruit, a tedious job, as we were to see later on, with the gardeners balanced carefully on ladders working often in bitter wind, arms raised above shoulder level, hands in mittens and drips continually falling from the tips of their noses. The sun, when it shone, cast long shadows even at mid-day, rising

Ken pruning the plum trees

not much higher than the garden walls and setting only just behind the western side of the church.

The harsh conditions also caused pigeons to start attacking the brassicas. Long lines of thin plastic tape were stretched from cane to cane (each 15 feet apart) along the rows of cabbages and sprouts; when the wind blew, the tapes uttered a terrible wailing sound, which they did to great effect, scaring the birds away and bringing a note of melancholy to a garden that already looked bleak enough.

Vegetables for the house this month were not very exciting – just leeks, cabbages, sprouts and roots, with a little cress sown in punnets and a few forced chicories to add to the salads. These were blanched in a specially designed pot in the warmest and darkest place of all, the mushroom shed. This is next to the mess room. It was specially designed for mushroom growing, as well as the

blanching of chicory and the forcing of
rhubarb, asparagus and sea kale. It has
no windows, just sliding shutters
over skylights in the wood-lined
ceiling. Mushrooms are no longer
grown here but the enormous slate
shelves that held their beds are still in
place. Each shelf is designed to be filled
with compost. Because of the great weight of this compost the
shelves are supported on hefty cast iron frames, with slots for slate
cills to retain the compost.

forced chicory

This shed, built by Messengers, might have succeeded an
older mushroom shed which was probably sited behind the old
greenhouses. I make this assumption because among the Langham
papers in the local Record Office there is a copy of Isaac Oldacre's
Receipt for Growing Mushrooms, written about 1800. Oldacre
practised this method in St Petersburg, where he was one of the
gardeners to the Czar of Russia. His mushroom house was built
very similarly to Messengers'. His instructions for the compost
were that the shelves should be filled with a compact mass of fresh
horse dung and straw, beaten 'as close together as possible'. When
it was six inches deep the surface was smoothed off. As soon as the
compost was 'as warm as milk from the cow' natural fermentation
holes were made in it with a dibble to receive the mushroom
spawn. When the heat declined the spawn was inserted and
covered with more dung, the whole bed being finished off with an
inch and a half of yet more dung. (In the summer, mushrooms
might appear without the insertion of spawn.) The beds were
beaten down again and 'finished off for good'. If necessary they
were lightly watered. The room was kept at 55°F. Impregnated
beds, if kept dry, lasted for years according to Oldacre. They could
be re-activated whenever mushrooms were required by covering
them with fresh dung.

To make briquettes of spawn there was a simple method,
similar (but only in one respect) to that of making yoghurt. The
culture is encouraged by heat. Equal amounts of fresh horse
droppings and cow, deer or sheep manure were mixed with 'a
sufficient portion of earth or road-sand to cement it together'. This
was mashed well into a compost, spread on the floor of an open
shed and left until it was firm enough to shape into square bricks.
When half dry three walnut-sized holes were dibbled in each brick
and filled with pieces of 'good old spawn'. The bricks were left a
few days to settle, then heaped into a pile three feet wide on top of a
bed of dry horse dung six inches deep. The bricks, arranged in a

ridge-shaped line, were then covered with fresh warm horse dung 'sufficient in quantity to diffuse a gentle glow through the whole bed'. The spawn spread in this way through every part of each brick. When the process was finished the bricks were kept in a dry place, to be used as required. Spawn was originally collected in the autumn from pastures where mushrooms grew naturally. A crop could be induced to grow on beds of horse dung, but only for a limited time out of doors. Oldacre's method provided mushrooms all the year round.

The temperature is usually between 70° and 75°F in the winter in Doug's mushroom house, which makes it quite cosy. Fortunately one of the most boring January jobs, the washing of countless flower pots, is done in here, usually by Joy. Here too, under

weed-killing sprayer

lock and key, Doug keeps all his chemicals for the many sprays and potions he uses throughout the year. After seeing all these poisons, and noting the frequency with which they were applied, I asked Doug several months later why he used them. He said he'd much rather not, but because the farmland all round him is so heavily treated with chemical pesticides and weedkillers his gardens had become a sort of sanctuary for every kind of bug, fly, rot and 'noxious pest'. There was no answer to this problem except to use the same sprays as the farmers. I had also noticed a fairly heavy reliance on chemical fertilisers. Doug disliked them too, knowing that farmyard manure and compost gave far better results, but once again economics and modern farming methods were against him. Weedkillers used by the Home Farm were sometimes still active in the strawy parts of the manure sent to the gardens, which could put kitchen garden plants at risk as we were to find out, later in the year. These days there was certainly no likelihood of mushrooms appearing spontaneously, as they used to, in manure or pasture.

As for compost, in spite of a gigantic dump, just outside the frame yard, of discarded pot plants, garden rubbish and the trimmings from all the vegetables sent to the Hall, there was simply not enough time, Doug said, to give it all the turning, aerating, watering and attention that is required to process it into proper garden compost.

In the vinery the pruned, knobbly vine rods had been lowered on strings from the top of the house. They usually grow at an angle of 45° to the ground; they were now in a horizontal position. There are two reasons for this. First, the run of sap is easier, which leads to earlier growth; second, with the rods lowered Ken can more easily reach them to strip off the old bark and paint them with his particular mixture of insecticide. In the old days the stripped rods would have been 'thoroughly cleansed with soap and water, then painted over with a thick coating of equal parts of sulphur, soot, lime and cowdung, made into a paste with strong soap suds' (*Beeton's New Book of Garden Management*, 1885). Ken uses a mixture of nicotine, tar oil and Rovral. In January the vines show no signs of life at all, though the fig, which has also been sprayed with tar oil, had tiny green bumps along its otherwise naked branches.

This month is the start of the seed-sowing season. The propagation house (average temperature 60° to 75°F) was completely cleared and smoked (fumigated) at the start of January in preparation for the arrival of countless pans, trays, boxes and pots. All the gardeners take a hand in mixing composts in the potting shed.

They are given three different and strictly secret formulas for three sorts of compost – 'seed', 'potting' and 'final'; their making seems to me to be very like mixing the dry ingredients for a cake. Once made up, the composts are stored under the bench in large sacks. Secrecy is traditional; head gardeners are notoriously jealous of their own composts.

Doug says anyone can sow the outdoor seeds but, again by tradition, only the head gardener is allowed to sow the indoor

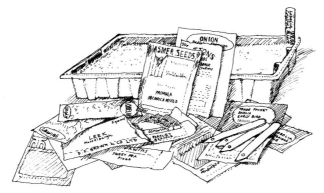

Doug's February seed packets

seeds, which is to say seeds that need hothouse propagation. These are usually the seeds of the more expensive or delicate plants so that if none comes up, or if anything goes wrong there is no excuse, and the head gardener can blame no one but himself. Most of the enormous December delivery of seeds was sown by the end of January. At the end of each week Doug wrote down in his journal everything he had sown. He explained that each sort of seed needed different depths, spacing and compost. I suspect that another reason for his insistence on sowing seeds himself is that the seed trays need to be labelled with the names spelt both correctly and legibly. The list of seeds sown just in the last week of January is as follows:

Cape gooseberry	Leptospermum scorparium (mixed)
Asclepias 'Gay Butterfly'	Crossandra infundibuliformis
Asclepias curassavica	Euphorbia millii splendens
Tecoma stans	Albizia julibrissin
Zantedeschia (new hybrids)	Alstroemeria pulchella
Chamaecyparis funebris	Gentian lutea
Cupressus cashmeriana	Primula candelabra (hybrid)
Ornithogalum candidum	Primula waltonii (hybrid)
Boronia pinnata	Eryngium alpinum
Boronia megastigma	Eryngium (mixed)
Abutilon bella (mixed)	Primula melanops
Pentas (dwarf hybrids)	Geranium (garden spp. mixed)

The seed-sowing process (which continues well into March) has something of a religious rite about it. Doug seats himself at the potting shed bench on a stool, while Ken or Joy stand by like acolytes. He throws a measure of the correct compost on to the

young cineraria
(dark purple)

The fig pruned with lowered vine rods beyond

bench and packs it into a number of seed trays. He carefully taps the seed from its packet, covers it with more compost shaken through an old kitchen sieve, tamps it down with a board made just to fit the tray and labels it neatly with a new label – never with an old one as that might carry disease. Ken or Joy carry the trays into the propagation house. Neither of them makes any attempt to pronounce the names on the labels, and Jess, who spends much of his time taking carnation, chrysanthemum or fuschia cuttings, says he's never heard of half the things Doug grows.

The big event this month was the Hunt Ball on January 26. The meet was held at the Hall in the morning – the Ball was held at a nearby mansion that night. Doug supplied cut flowers and seventy-one pot plants for this event. Plants for the Hall this month were mostly cyclamen, calceolarias, cineraria, *Primula obconica*, *Primula kewensis* and flowering bulbs such as hyacinths, narcissi and daffodils. Cut flowers include daffodils, carnations, echevarias, gerberas, geraniums, the first arum lilies and the last chrysanthemums.

What with the fragrance of the flowering bulbs in the vinery and the mild weather at the end of the month, the gardeners might well have had a feeling that winter was over. Alas, the worst was yet to come.

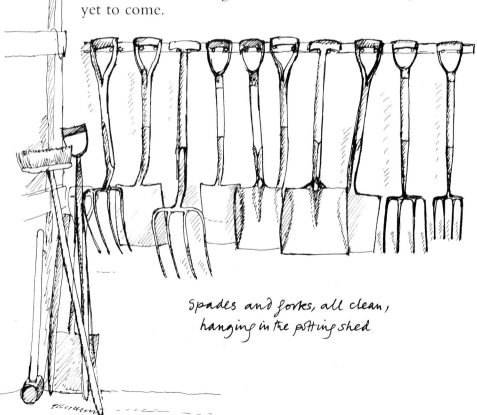

Spades and forks, all clean,
hanging in the potting shed

FEBRUARY

Fifth visit Monday, 18 February 1985

Neither of us has visited the gardens since before Christmas. We feel so frustrated by this that, even though most of the country is thickly covered with snow, we set off for Cottesbrooke regardless of the state of the roads. It is a fine, clear day.

In the orchard the pruned apple trees show up darkly against the snow, their branches have lost last year's straggly growth. They have all been sprayed with tar oil. The prunings are being burnt with some old pea sticks and bean poles in a lovely bonfire; Teresa and John are spending the morning feeding them into the smoke.

Doug's news, though, is of nothing but disasters; on February 8 they had such low temperatures and such a heavy fall of snow that the village was snowbound. There were ten-foot drifts on the main road running along the high ridge to the east of Cottesbrooke; the lanes surrounding the village were narrowed to a single track; even the drive to the Hall was blocked by snowdrifts, an inconvenience that Doug only discovered after he had walked to the Hall across the park to check the décor because his van's battery was flat. On that occasion the temperature was −10°C at seven in the morning.

The bad weather gave Doug the opportunity to set his staff on to the indoor tasks such as washing the glasshouses, oiling all locks and bolts, clearing the store rooms and checking all the fruit in store. He was also able to give most of his outside gardeners, Ken, Sid, Jess and himself, holidays that were due to them thanks to a rearrangement of time off by the Estate Manager. Fuel began to run low and he reduced the boiler temperature; old as they are, these boilers continually supply their equally antiquated pump with water at a temperature of around 180°F, which falls to about 70°F by the time it returns, but the fuel consumption by the pair of them is immense when the weather is cold. Doug's journal records a delivery of 3,200 litres of Diesella fuel oil in December, another 3,760 litres in January and, with only 120 gallons left in the tank, another 3,600 litres followed by 3,200 litres this month. 3,600 litres, I note, costs £1,147.

On Monday February 11 he observed that 300 gallons had been used over the weekend; temperatures had ranged from a minimum of −12°C to a maximum of −5°C for over a week, but he had managed to keep the fig house at 4°C (this is always the coolest house); the propagation house (the hottest) never went below 20°C. All the same the bitter cold and constant east wind killed almost all his sprouts and all his Savoys, winter cabbage, sprouting broccoli and early cauliflowers. They

frosted Brussels sprouts stand as withered and wilted stumps in the garden, a sad sight.

The only vegetables to survive are the leeks, swedes, parsnips, kale, 'January King' cabbages, red cabbages, the stored onions, the potatoes and carrots stored in the sheds and the potatoes and carrots in the clamps. Most of the time though, the ground was too frozen to lift the leeks, swedes or parsnips, which left very little for him to send to the Hall.

The frost on the cold frames had also been intense; their covers of carpet and sacking froze on to the glass and the lights themselves froze so hard to the frames that they couldn't be opened for over a week. However, all the liliums, hydrangeas and early chrysanthemum stools inside survived this ordeal. The snow actually acts as insulation; today Ken is brushing it off some empty frames before filling them with more seed trays.

The presence of an ice-house between the lodge gates and the Grange reminds me that at this time of the year, or as soon as any nearby pond or water had frozen over, the gardeners would have been fully employed in collecting ice and snow to replenish last year's stores. The entrance to the ice-house at Cottesbrooke is bricked up now, and its pond (clearly shown on all the maps until 1900) has been drained. The ice-house itself might well be as old as the mansion; ice-houses were introduced to England in the reign of Charles II, whose own ice-house was the cause, when it was installed at Windsor on 23 April 1667, of a celebratory banquet at which cherries, strawberries and ice-creams were served. The invention of refrigerators in the mid-nineteenth century relieved gardeners of the annual task of collecting ice and snow and gradually made ice-houses redundant.

There is a problem with water for the poly tunnel too. All the garden taps are frozen; the only ones working are those some

The orchard under snow

distance off by the greenhouses, which have been kept unfrozen by the hot water pipes. A great snake of hose leads from one of these taps to the tunnel, which is filled with a fine mist. The tunnel is watered by sprays fixed in an overhead pipe that runs along its length. The crops in here are growing well; the peas and broad beans are now almost four inches high, there are six rows of infant lettuces, one row of parsley, four dozen young cauliflowers and two rows of radishes just showing their leaves, as well as a fair-sized patch of flourishing young strawberry plants; their tender, vigorous growth gives no hint whatsoever of the harsh conditions outside.

The same delicious impression of expansion and warmth is to be felt in the vinery. Here, tiny leaflets on the vines provide evidence that the sap is indeed now running fast along the still lowered rods. The fig branches are also breaking out in little leaves. Most exciting of all is the nectarine beside the fig which has

pricking out, seed trays
on the potting shed bench

started to flower; its branches are dotted from trunk to tip with delicate pink buds and tiny, bright-green leaves. The colour and scent of the flowering pot plants in the vinery only add to the illusion that spring has come. There are orange clivias and strelizias, yellow daffodils and white narcissi, dark pink azaleas, tubs of climbing, flowering jasmine, cinerarias of every hue from purple to crimson to white and bowls of dark-blue hyacinths. The heat from the sun is actually so strong that all the hothouse plants have needed watering several times in the past two weeks and the game of chess, played by moving plants from one house or frame to another, has intensified to such a pitch that I suspect only Doug knows where everything is.

Many of the seeds sown last month are now seedlings, some of which need pricking out into more boxes, pans, trays and pots.

The scale on which these gardens operate can now be guessed at by looking in the cold frames, heated frames and propagation house and reading the data in Doug's journal: '8 Feb. pricked out onions into seed trays 20 x 60, vars. Ailsa Craig and Wijbo; 12 Feb. pricked out 13 x 48 trays African marigold; 14 Feb. started pricking out Cabbage Golden Acre into trays 6 x 60; 15 Feb. pricked out into trays 4 x 60 Cabbage Golden Acre also into 3½" pots put Asclepias curasavica, Tecoma stans, Cape gooseberry, Albizia julibrissin, Gerbera Mardi Gras', etc.

The pricking out is usually done by Joy, each box ending up with multiples of four, five or six. She says she enjoys it. She sits all morning in the potting shed, delicately transferring each tiny seedling from its original, crowded seed tray with the aid of a pointed stick and dropping it into a neat hole in its new tray. Each pricked-out seedling forms part of a dotted green grid. Her previous job, she tells me, was equally finicky; it was making car-harnesses for Rovers in an electrical factory.

At the other end of the potting shed Jess is just as patiently reglazing and painting some old-fashioned lantern cloches. They are made of small panes of glass set into iron frames. Huge bell-shaped glasses (hence the name 'cloche') were used by gardeners before the invention, early in the eighteenth century, of lantern cloches. The lantern cloches had the advantage of being repairable if the glass broke. They were also easier to ventilate than the bell-glasses, though these continued to be used as well. Jess has eleven lantern cloches to deal with. He gets through two a day.

His cloches (which should be more properly called hand glasses) could be at least 100 years old; their frames are made of cast-iron. They have a square base with a removable lid shaped like a pyramid: a handle is fixed to the top. Loudon's gardening encyclopaedia of 1830 illustrates one exactly like Jess's, if a little more squat, and says of it '. . . each side is cast separate . . . and the top which is always kept separable is cast in one piece. When air is to be given to the plants enclosed, it is done by lifting up the top, and replacing it diagonally, by which means air is admitted in every

old-fashioned cloche

direction; and one advantage of not being obliged to lift the bottom part is that in severe weather, when it is frozen to the ground, air is admitted without danger of breaking the glass; add also that the leaves of large plants, as of cauliflower, are less liable to be injured in replacing it.' Loudon's hand glasses were fastened together with screws and nuts; Jess's slot into one another and can be fastened with wires. They will be used later on in the year, to protect the seedling courgettes.

Some 160 different sorts of seed have been sown by Doug in the past five weeks and the job is not finished yet. This month's selection includes celery, tomatoes, melons, Brussels sprouts and rhubarb, as well as the usual hothouse and bedding plants. He has also taken delivery of 217 kilos of seed potatoes, of which 49 kilos are first earlies, 43 kilos are early main crop and 125 kilos are main crop. These are being set to chit (sprout) in boxes under pieces of old carpet in the fruit store, which is now only partially full, most of the fruit having been eaten.

Before leaving, I make a note of the flowers and pot plants being sent to the Hall this month. The cut flowers are: daffodils, narcissi, arum lilies, carnations, gerberas and freesias. The pot plants are: cineraria, calceolaria, cyclamen, *Primula obconica, Primula malacoides, Primula sinensis*, blue and white browallias, ferns, *Begonia metallica, Cupressus funebris,* anigozanthus, *Azalea indica*, flowering jasmine, daffodils and hyacinths.

In comparison with the plants the choice of vegetables and fruit is rather dull and ordinary, but Doug reminds me that so much of last summer's produce was canned or frozen that they are probably eating peas, beans, raspberries and peaches as well as today's cabbages and parsnips.

We leave early. Before we finally make for home the car has to be towed out of a snowdrift by a tractor.

arum lilies

Nectarine blossom in full flower

MARCH

Sixth visit Wednesday, 27 March 1985

Because of the bitter weather in February the gardeners were forced to concentrate on work indoors. The start of March found the sheds, stores and offices even tidier than usual, with every tool and piece of machinery immaculately cleaned, repaired and oiled. It was mid-March before the Top and Middle Gardens at last received some attention; outdoor digging was and still is the main job; it has been continuous for the past two weeks. (The last of the wall fruit was pruned, sprayed and tied in at the start of the month.) The weather in March has not been that good either. According to Doug's journal, light snow and frost alternated with rain and bitter cold most of the time, with the result that all growth is very retarded. On Thursday March 21 Doug wrote: 'Frost and slight snow again o/night. Rained 7 pm 1st day of spring but bitterly cold, we are at least two weeks later this year than last.' For example, there is no sign yet of any outdoor blossom, not even on the south-facing walls, where the peaches, cherries, apricots and plums would be the first of the wall-fruit trees to flower. 'Just as well', Doug says, 'as they might very well get frosted if they blossom too soon.'

Ken and John taking potatoes from the clamp

Outdoor peach tree, pruned but not yet in flower

We are beginning to get into quite a routine with our visits now, driving directly to the business end of the gardens by the row of buildings that houses the potting shed, boiler room and mushroom house, rather than starting from Doug and Joy's front parlour as we did at first.

As soon as we find Doug he brings us up to date and gives us all the latest news, walking us through each of the hothouses, quartering both the Top and Middle Gardens and, if necessary, taking us into the orchard as well. The first news on this visit, which is over a month after the previous one, is that they have begun to use potatoes from the clamp and that they were all in perfect condition. About a third of the six or seven tons stored in the 30-foot-long clamp has already been taken, not entirely by the Hall. The best-run gardens inevitably grow more produce than they need from time to time; Cottesbrooke is no exception. The rule here, as in Evelyn's time, is that the surplus can be sold, although, as Evelyn says, the gardener 'may not dispose of any . . . Fruite nor sell any Artichock, Cabbages, Asparagus, Melons, Strawberries, Raspberries, Wall, or standard & dwarfe fruite, Roses, Violets, Cloves [carnations], or any Greenes [evergreens], or other flowers or plants, without first asking, and having leave of his Master or Mistress; nor till there be of sufficient of all garden furniture for the Grounds stock and families use.'

Doug's sales from the garden are all handled by the Estate Office. He has already sold eight hundredweight of potatoes to the itinerant greengrocer. Nine and a half hundredweight more have been put into the store under straw. John is bundling more potatoes into a sack. They look as good as they did on the day they were harvested six months ago; only the straw has changed, darkening and decaying a little with the damp. This excellent method of storing potatoes looks as antique and primitive as the salting or smoking of meat and fish and has for me much the same appeal, requiring as it does nothing but natural materials – earth and straw – to make it work. It needs none of today's gadgetry, machinery, fuel or power to keep it going.

three surviving swedes

The same could also be said, in part, of the poly tunnel. It is several degrees warmer in there today than it is outside. Here the radishes are ready to eat, a row of carrots is already showing feathery leaves and the peas and beans are a good six inches higher than they were last time we saw them. Four rows of early potatoes ('Dunluce') were planted here earlier in the month, to be ready for lifting, Doug hopes, by late May or early June.

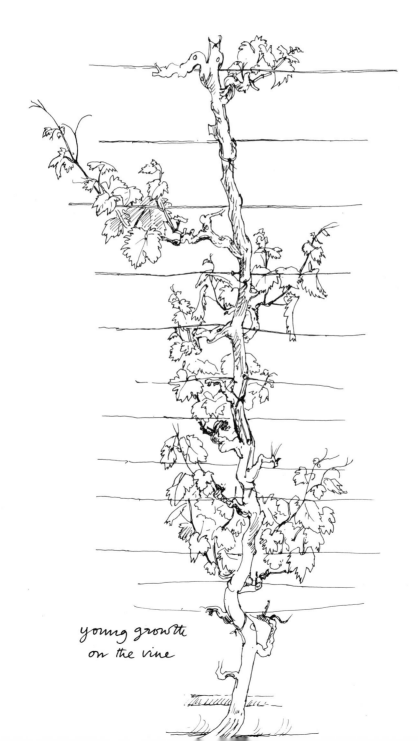

young growth on the vine

There is a greater contrast, though, between the cold, exposed gardens and the hot, sheltered greenhouses, where both machinery and fuel have been used to the fullest extent. Out of doors branches are still bare and the only things to be newly planted in these two acres of freshly dug ground are onions and shallots. A few leeks, cabbages, kales, sprouts, parsnips and swedes have come through the cold spell, but they look more dead than alive. However, even from a distance we can see that the vinery is filled with a bright green flush of new leaves. The rods are raised back to their proper position in the roof and are sending out crisp new shoots; some are only four or five inches long, others have reached two or three feet. Ken has started tying them into the wires that run along the roof at right angles to the rods. The force of the sap is so strong he has to be careful not to snap the shoots; he therefore only does this job on cold days when the pressure of sap is lower. His work is gradual but constant as the tender young branches grow almost visibly; he stops them two leaves after two potential bunches have appeared. Below the vines along the entire length of the house clivias, azaleas, arum lilies, pots of tulips and regal pelargoniums are all in flower, as are the tubs of forced potatoes planted in January and a small pot of wisteria trained round tall canes. Most spectacular of all is the peach blossom which now covers every twig and branch of half a dozen trees. It looks almost artificial, as if it were made of silk or feathers; the flowers grow in masses, closely together, and are prettily interspersed with tiny, bright-green, pointed leaves.

The house is allowed to breathe every day now; ventilators running the length of the ridge of the roof are raised or lowered by means of well-greased rods, cogs and cranks. It seems miraculous that they still work after seventy-odd years, but they are well designed, well made and well maintained. Doug has a copy of Messengers' catalogue of horticultural buildings (fifth edition, 1928) in his office, which illustrates a vinery exactly like his, and a peach house. The specifications for the ventilators are as follows: 'Roof ventilators [are] hung to ridge with purpose-made malleable iron hinges of the hook-and-eye type, which cannot wear, break, or be set fast by rust; and a fillet or bead fitting in a groove in the ridge cap effectually keeps out the weather. NB – In this connection it may be interesting to state that this weathering fillet was introduced in the year 1858, [the year of the firm's foundation] together with the special hinges referred to for the roof and front ventilators, and both are still in use today, nothing having been

young leaves, fig

68

A heated frame full of pricked-out seedlings

invented since which can in any way supersede or, indeed, approach them for efficiency.'

One of the advantages of the open ventilator is that if it is a warm day the bees come in, helping Doug with the task of pollinating the peaches, which he has been doing every day with the aid of the rabbit's tail on its cane. 'Another way', he tells us, 'is simply to bang the main branches and shake the pollen off'; this is best done at mid-day when the pollen becomes looser.

The figs left on the tree last winter are beginning to swell. The nectarine beside the fig tree, which flowered so early, is now setting fruit; this will be left to grow until May or June when the stones begin to form, and then it will be thinned.

Also seen in the vinery: cucumbers and tomatoes already inches high, in gro-bags, and pots of young sweet peas ranged all along the shelves above our heads. More tomatoes and cucumbers have been planted out in the lean-to greenhouse in the Top Garden.

The propagation house is half empty again. I wonder how many seed trays have been taken in and out of this neat, warm clean place since the New Year? As soon as the seedlings are big enough they are pricked out by Joy and placed in the cold frames to harden off. The game of chess is endless. It is almost as if the gardens had a pulse of their own that never stops beating. Several boxes of hardened-off perennial plants have gone to the Hall gardens (aubretia, pink arabis, white arabis and sweet Williams) to make more room for the new boxes. Today the propagation house shelters begonia tubers, tomato seedlings and melon seedlings. Dozens more packets of seed have been sown this month. Of fruit and vegetable seed alone Doug has sown:

> cucumber ('Athene')
> celery ('Giant White' and 'Celebrity')
> leek ('Alma' and 'Giant Winter')
> capsicum ('Cleo' and 'Canape F1')
> celeriac
> red cabbage
> Brussels sprout ('Early Half Tall')
> aubergine ('Slice Rite 23')
> cauliflower ('Veitch's sp.' and 'Royal Purple')
> melon ('Emerald Gem')
> lettuce ('Great Lakes', 'Little Gem', 'Nabucco' and 'Salad Bowl')
> broccoli ('Calabrese Green Sprouting' and 'Romanesco')
> Savoy cabbage
> tomato ('Ailsa Craig')
> French beans ('Sunray')

Doing in the potting shed, sowing seeds

Cuttings have been taken of chrysanthemums, dahlias, fuchsias, helichrysums and carnations. Fifty-two packets of seed of herbaceous plants, pot plants and exotics have also been sown, ranging alphabetically from *Adenophora liliflora* to zinnia ('Yoga' mixed). A box of chrysanthemum cuttings is shaded by sheets of newspaper in case the sun is too hot; seed pans containing nicotiana, broccoli, celery and lettuce are covered by panes of glass to conserve moisture. They are removed as soon as the microscopic green dots of germinated seed appear. Both the heated and the cold frames are filled to capacity with boxes of infant plants. Last time we came the cold frames were hidden under wraps which were frozen solid to the lights. Now each frame has a cast-off heap of old sacks and bits of carpet lying beside it; the covers will be replaced in the last half-hour before home-going time.

The pricking out, taking of cuttings, potting up and potting on has been so relentless that Joy has asked Doug to see if the estate carpenter can make her a higher stool to sit on while she works.

Just before we leave Ken spots mealy bugs on his vines. They must have survived the lethal mixture he was painting on the rods in January. Now, because so many vulnerable plants are occupying the space below the vines, he will have to use methylated spirits. 'It's us against them!' shouts Doug, quite cheerfully for once. The colour of the methylated spirits matches Ken's jersey exactly. The methylated spirits undoubtedly acts as an insecticide but it forms no sort of preventive. It seems more likely that the constant brushing of the crevices in which the mealy bugs and their eggs are found is the best way to get rid of them, or at least to reduce their numbers. Loudon, whose common sense illuminates every page of the 1830 edition of his *Encyclopaedia of Gardening*, says of the mealy bug, or as he calls it, the *coccus genus*, 'Brushing off these creatures is the only effectual remedy, and, if set about at once and persevered in, will save the trouble of many prescribed washes and powders, which are mere palliatives.' Among those palliatives, Charles MacIntosh, one of his contemporaries, recommended the introduction of an 'ammoniacal gas' by continually watering and turning a ridge of fresh unfermented horse manure inside the length of the vinery or, if 'neatness and order are a consideration' and the 'not very agreeable appearance' and the 'much less pleasant smell' were objected to, a substitute could be made 'by pouring a solution of crude muriate of ammonia upon quick lime, and the gas thus obtained may be applied with a pair of bellows to the plants'. Sir Joseph Banks recommended scrubbing the branches with a hard brush and strong lime-water; later Victorians such as James Anderson advised 'painting the affected

clivias growing in a pot

parts with paraffine', but added, 'It is better in all cases to deal with the insect timeously, otherwise a general washing with such a powerful searching liquid might prove fatal to the life of the tree.'

Before we leave I make a note of the cut flowers and pot plants sent to the Hall this month. They are: daffodils, arum lilies, freesias, carnations, gerberas, clivias and odontoglossums (orchids) as cut flowers; cinerarias, narcissi, hyacinths, flowering wisterias and jasmine, *Primula kewensis* and *Primula obconica* as pot plants. (Ken puts little cushions of moss in each of the hyacinth bowls before they are taken to the house.) Azaleas, hydrangeas, achimenes (hot-water plants), geraniums and regal pelargoniums are now being forced for next month's décor. One more extra job for Doug (taken from his journal): 'Potted into 3″ net pots 60 sweet Williams and some pansies for sale at Fund Raising Function [Conservative Association's Easter Fair].'

clivia flower-head

APRIL

Seventh visit Friday, 19 April 1985

Easter was two weeks ago. Today the weather is beautiful, spring-like and balmy. The blossom has burst on all the outdoor peaches, gages and apricots; the almost imperceptible green flowers of the red currants and gooseberries are just beginning to open. Polyanthuses and forget-me-nots are flowering in the corner bed at the entrance to the frame yard.

The poly tunnel has the temperature and atmosphere of a Turkish bath. John and Teresa are weeding in there, wearing only T-shirts, jeans and running shoes. They are hoeing a foot-high canopy of chickweed from the surface of the warm, dry soil. Tomatoes and aubergines are to be planted here next. They also weed between the rows of lettuces (varieties 'Miranda' and 'Mayfair') which have become enormous. They are the pale-green floppy kind, similar to those sold in supermarkets but twice or three times the size. Teresa is amused that I should be so impressed by this. 'The reason they don't grow them as big as this for the shops', she says proudly, 'is that they couldn't fit them into those little plastic bags.' Doug, who has been selling these lettuces to the greengrocer for 12p a piece is astonished when I tell him that an iceberg lettuce in Marks and Spencer costs 70p at the moment.

As if to show off all its advantages, the broad beans and the peas in the poly tunnel are flowering and the early potatoes, planted six weeks earlier, are already earthed up.

skillet and dibber, planting out

All the outdoor potatoes are now planted and more outdoor sowing is in progress. Bare soil, neatly hoed, sown and raked, is punctuated only by Doug's labels: spinach, carrots, Texsel greens, onions, radishes, parsnips, more broad beans, more peas, cauliflowers, cabbages, sprouts, broccoli, kohlrabi and turnips. After lunch Teresa sows more carrots, stretching a line for guidance with a string wound round an iron reel. Doug calls this contraption a skillet. Teresa, who has lived here all her life, thinks it was made by George, the estate blacksmith, who died in 1980 aged 95. Once the line is in place she makes her drill with a hoe, taps in the seed from a packet, then covers the drill neatly again by drawing the forked end of the hoe along the line. She really prefers to shuffle along the row tipping the soil into the drill with her feet, then lightly treading it down, but Doug, acting with each of our visits more like a stage-manager than a gardener, insists she does it the proper way, at least while Hugh is photographing the process. 'Or you can do the old gardeners' trick with a rake,' he suggests, 'use the back to make wide drills and the side to make narrow ones. You fill them in in the same way, by drawing the rake from side to side on its back.'

In the Top Garden the plastic tapes set as pigeon scarers make an eerie sound like a gale blowing across moorland, but after the bitterly cold weather there are only a few rows of kale left standing. Out of the 480 broccolis planted last year, only 12 are still alive. Because the spring cabbage is so late this year the kitchen is actually buying greens, but yesterday the first bunch of asparagus was cut. Lettuces and blanched rhubarb are being sent as well. There are still plenty of leeks in the ground and there is still a supply of onions and roots stored in sheds. The carrots are still in the clamp, which is as yet unbroached. Doug opens it for us, starting at the top. They are as sweet, juicy and fresh as the day they went in six months ago; there are just a few pale-yellow shoots on their tops. The potato clamp is still in use and the potatoes are still being washed and bagged up for sale. Doug says this covers the cost of buying the seed, though he is not actually burdened with the need to make the gardens pay for themselves by selling their produce. The ground on which the potatoes grew last year is now being prepared for next winter's brassicas, which, as long as the weather is less cruel than this year, will see the kitchen through until next April.

The cut flowers for this month are much the same as last month: clivias, arums, freesias, daffodils and tulips. The pot plants are similar too; cinerarias, *Primula obconica, Primula kewensis,* winter-flowering begonias and calceolarias, plus regal pelargoniums, amaryllises and schizanthus.

Because it is so warm Ken and Doug are taking the lights (the window-like covers) off the cold frames. These frames can be partially ventilated by sliding the lights up or down, but for full ventilation the lights must be lifted right off. There are three rows of cold frames; 40 feet of wooden-based ones by the potting shed, another 30 feet, brick-based, at the further end of the hothouse range and a third (also 30 feet long and brick-based) against the fruit-room wall. All are full of hardy, over-wintered lettuces at the moment, of the same varieties as those in the poly tunnel but not so far advanced. Between them the cold frames add up to 100 feet of unheated shelter. Those with brick bases are 18 inches high in front and six feet across, rising to three feet at the back. The lights are large; each one measures six by four feet, contains 24 panes of glass and is designed to be lifted by two men; it takes both Ken and Doug to move them now. They are made of wood and are extremely heavy. Doug says they are called English lights. The more modern Dutch light, invented between the wars, is only five by two and a quarter feet. It can be easily lifted by one man as it is half the size of the English light and is made with only one large pane of glass. Doug would prefer Dutch lights, but their size is incompatible with the bases of the frames in this frame yard which was, after all, built before the First World War.

There is no lifting problem with the lights on the heated frames. There are two heated span frames, both 30 feet long and 10 feet wide, at either end of the range of span greenhouses. These are described in the sale catalogue of 1935 as heated plant pits, but the pits have been filled in to ground level since then. They both have ventilators running the length of the roof, worked by an ingenious crank at one end. The lights themselves are hinged at the tops and are propped open by smartly painted black iron bars. There are five more frames, not heated as such, but they take the benefit of the heat that comes through the ventilators of the walls against which they are built. These lean-to frames lie outside each of the peach houses, on either side of the palm house and on the western side of the carnation house. Each of these frames is 30 feet long and 6 feet wide. Between them they add up to 150 feet of warm frames, to which Doug can add the 60 feet of heated frames. In the summer the lights of these frames act as shades for the plants inside and are either painted with opaque green 'Summer Cloud', or are covered with blinds made of thin slats of wood.

The use of frames is ancient. They were first made to shelter plants growing on hot beds. Hot beds are described by gardening writers as long ago as the eleventh century. They were made very

Azalea and nectarine in flower

ventilator winch, peach house

simply by heaping fresh stable manure into low, flat heaps. The fresh manure fermented and therefore heated up. The beds were then covered, once the first great heat had abated, with a depth of soil sufficient for whatever was to be grown in it. The heat was maintained by periodically lining the outside of the bed with fresh manure. The Tudors used hot beds for melons, early salads and early peas. Later gardeners used them for any vegetable suitable for forcing, including potatoes, sea kale, French beans, herbs (particularly mint) and asparagus, as well as spring bulbs and flowers.

The Tudors merely sheltered their hot beds with 'tabernacles' of sail cloth, old picture canvases or straw matting, suspended over the plants on an arrangement of forked twigs, hoops of wood, or struts resembling table legs. These coverings had to be taken off whenever the sun shone. The invention, in the seventeenth century, of bell-glasses (or cloches) was a great improvement, as they allowed light to reach each of the plants they protected. The only drawback with glasses was that it was necessary to tilt them or remove them completely in order to avoid cooking the plants with a build-up of steam, or burning them with a concentration of the sun's rays. Framed 'lights', placed just inside the top of the hot bed, were eventually thought of; the hot bed was built as before so that it and the tops of the frames sloped towards the south to catch the heat of the sun (the slope also drained off any wet). At first the wooden frames were covered with 'moveable lights' or windows made of oiled paper. Later the lights were made of panes of glass. Brick pits containing hot dung or fermenting tanner's bark were a development of the hot bed; they were originally designed for growing the first English pineapples early in the eighteenth century. They were covered in exactly the same way as hot beds, with brick or wooden frames and transparent lights. Hot beds only went out of use with the improvements brought about by the invention of pipes carrying steam, hot air or hot water, but the proportions of the old hot beds remain: six feet across or the reach, from either side, of a man's arm and any length you wish as long as it is divisible by four, four feet being the width of each light.

Like the cold frames and the hothouses, the heated frames, both span and lean-to, were built by Messengers and are illustrated in their catalogue. According to their specifications these frames

Jess replacing vinery glass

are all made from 'two inch good quality Red Deal, thoroughly well seasoned'. They are fitted with iron strengthening bars and handles and were originally glazed with 21-ounce glass 'bedded in putty and well sprigged, and [the wood] painted three coats'. Jess, who is chiefly responsible for reglazing, painting and maintaining the glasshouses and frames, finds that glass of many different weights has been used for repairs since then, not all of it suitable, 'especially that thin war-time stuff'.

Jess would enjoy reading Charles MacIntosh on the subject of glass for hothouses. In 1828 he wrote, in his *Practical Gardener and Modern Horticulturist*: 'It is necessary that all hot-houses should be glazed with the best crown glass, as admitting a greater share of light to the plants contained therein, and not with glass of an inferior quality, as was long the practice ... It appears, by the experiments of Bouguer, that one-fortieth part of the light, which falls perpendicularly on the purest crystal, is reflected off, nor does it pass through it; it may be safely asserted, that green glass reflects off more than three-fourths. There is nothing gained by using bad glass in the glazing of hot-houses, but evidently much is lost.'

MacIntosh also recommends the use of what he calls the 'fragment form' of glass pane for frames. These rectangular frames have the lowest edge cut as a curve. They are still in use on the Cottesbrooke hothouses and frames. This shape of pane 'has this advantage, that it aids in conducting the water which falls on the roof to run down the centre of the pane, by which means, it is less likely to get into the house, between the glass and bars.'

This is the first visit on which we have spent more time outdoors than in, but Joy is still at her tasks in the potting shed, pricking out, potting on. She is sitting up on her new stool: 'Still not right', she says cheerfully, 'it's too tall.' Yesterday she and Doug manned the plant stall at the Hall for the Conservative Association's Bring and Buy coffee morning. 'All sold out in half-an-hour, making £83.55p and Doug had to answer questions all the time, like Gardeners' Questions on the radio.' Doug is sowing marrow seeds 'pointed end, look you, downwards, always'. His seed sowing for indoor propagation appears to be ceaseless. Thirty-four kinds of seed, including melons, cucumbers,

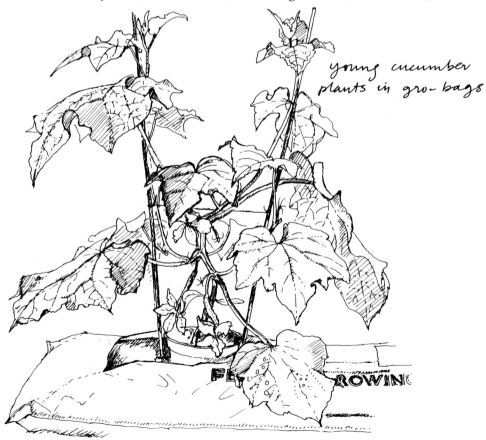

young cucumber plants in gro-bags

Plum tree in blossom, out of doors

bedding and hothouse plants, were sown in the first week of April alone. Today's batch finished, they are placed mostly in the heated frames as the propagation house has been given over to cucumbers and melons in bright-blue plastic gro-bags. The first batch of melons ('Blenheim Orange') was planted here a month ago. Doug grows two plants per bag; there is room for eight plants on each side of the house which, we see for the first time, has heavy benches made of thick, wide slabs of slate. By the beginning of July he hopes to have the first of 60 to 80 melons, as each plant will be expected to produce at least four fruits. Today he is planting out a later variety, 'Emerald Gem'. The roof is quite naked at the moment except for sheets of opaque white polythene shading in the cucumber half of the house. Soon, he says, it will be covered with melon and cucumber vines, meeting at the top from either side.

Spring appears to have been and gone in the vinery; the clivias have finished flowering. In the peach houses all the blossom has vanished, the leaves are almost fully grown and the fruit has set well. The infant peaches are a silver, furry pale green; the nectarines are a darker, shiny green. The figs that will form the first crop are quite large; a second crop is already beginning to grow and on the vines sprays of what will eventually be grapes are elegantly silhouetted against their light-green leaves and the blue sky above the vinery glass. There are ten pots of forced French beans on the vinery shelves; they should be ready to eat in late June. The earliest tomatoes are flowering in the Top Garden's greenhouse and the forced potatoes growing in tubs will be ready at the end of next month. All the ventilators are open; summer's overtime begins now. There will be watering to do around 6 pm (after tea) and the ventilators must then be closed. This is a chore that can last another three hours in hot weather, but it makes up for all those weeks of going home early in the winter.

Can winter really be over? The coverings on the cold frames seem to have been discarded; Doug's journal says the weather is mainly mild and sunny, but there are still night frosts and, as yet, there is no sign of blossom in the apple orchard or on the pears against the north walls. Hugh wants to take a photograph of this. 'Come back in two or three weeks', Doug advises, 'it's bound to be out by then'.

pot-grown potatoes, flowering

Peach fruit starting to set

M A Y

Eighth visit Wednesday, 15 May 1985

So far, May has been much colder than April; as a result our special trip for taking the apple blossom photographs has been delayed. We waited for almost four weeks rather than the two or three that Doug had supposed it might take for the orchard to come into full flower. Even now it looks as if we are going to be disappointed. Early on Monday Doug said he thought the trees would be ready by Wednesday, but Monday and Tuesday were bitterly cold and wet. Today, Wednesday, is cold and grey; the buds, ready to burst open at the first touch of sun, are still tightly shut. It is early, only 9.30 am, when we arrive, but the weather shows no signs of improving.

Plenty of other things have happened though: both the potato and the carrot clamps have gone and the straw protecting them has been taken to the dump. All the potatoes have been sold. The rain, unfortunately, got into the carrot clamp after Doug opened it up for us on our last visit and spoiled much of it.

The immature peaches have been thinned. They are now about the size of walnuts, still green with shiny silver fur, but more spaced out along their branches. Each fruit is about four inches apart from the next; before they were thinned they grew in clusters of two or three. Doug and Ken are thinning nectarines this morning. The earliest tree (not, oddly enough, the first one to flower but another variety in the hotter of the two peach houses) already has coloured fruit on it, almost ripe. Some of the branches bearing peaches and nectarines are really no more than twigs, not nearly strong enough to take the weight of the fruit when it ripens. Ken is therefore tying the ends of these twigs to the supporting wires which run horizontally behind the trees on the back wall and across the trellises at the front of the houses. Each fruit, when ripe, could weigh four to six ounces. The peach tree labelled 'Lord Napier' is now partially thinned; the moment to do this, Doug tells me, is as soon as the stone inside the fruit has fully formed. 'Once the stone has formed, the fruit seems to stand still for about two weeks not growing, not ripening. Then it gets moving and begins

Young seedlings and an old plum tree

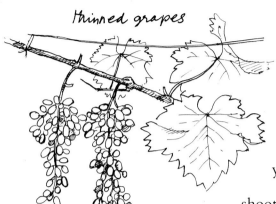

thinned grapes

to swell. From this time on it will bruise if it's touched, even if it's still green' – this is how that lady visitor did her damage last year on an Open Day, by handling the green fruit. Doug predicts that there will be a good crop of peaches this year. Last year they picked over 600.

On each of the hundreds of vine shoots there are now two delicate, pale-green sprays of vine flowers. The earliest black grape, 'Madresfield Court', shows signs of a good crop and has already set its fruit. Ken started thinning it on Monday, starting at 9.30 in the morning and finishing at half-past four. In that time he thinned twenty bunches; we work out that each bunch took about twenty minutes to do. He continues this task after lunch; it looks even more tedious and uncomfortable than pruning, as most of the branches are above his head and the work is slow and intricate. As soon as each baby grape is touching its neighbour thinning has to begin. Dozens of pea-sized green berries will have to be removed from each bunch. The tools for thinning are a short, thin stick sharpened to a point and a pair of vinery scissors with long handles and short, sharp, pointed blades. With the stick Ken lifts the clusters of immature grapes so that his scissors can work without damaging the berries. Taking care to keep each bunch a good shape he snips off about half the fruit. This allows the rest of the fruit to swell to a larger size than it would do otherwise. It also reduces the risk of mould. By the end of the operation what was a tight, compact green bunch is now a shapely cluster, with light and air round each berry and a heap of the thinned berries lying on a sack spread out beneath Ken's ladder. He says people used to make wine from the thinnings, in which case they must have added a great deal of sugar. I ask him if he has ever heard of verjuice, a sharp and useful liquid tasting like vinegar, made from green grapes, but he has not. It is a common ingredient in Tudor cookery books; it probably began to go out of favour

grape-thinning scissors

when sugar became easier to buy. (I have also read of the thinnings being used to make tarts, but this seems to have gone out of fashion too.)

As he works Ken notices more mealy bug on his vines, which means another session with the paint brush and methylated spirits. There are about twelve different varieties of grape in Ken's vinery (six being recently planted by Doug) and I begin to think, he must be familiar with every inch of every one of them. The vinery roof is almost covered now with their leaves and branches.

'Cambridge Favourite'

In the poly tunnel the cauliflower plants are already half their full size; they have made tremendous growth since we were here last. The strawberries have finished flowering and are actually ripening. The dwarf broad beans are flowering and the peas are bushing out around their supporting sticks; none is yet quite big enough to pick. John digs up a few of the potatoes in the tunnel, but they are not quite ready yet either, a meagre show. The gigantic lettuces have nearly all been cleared. Teresa is cutting and packing them for sale, still at 12p each, six heads to a box, each box lined with clean white tissue paper taken from a ream in Doug's office cupboard.

The potatoes that were being forced in tubs in the vinery were turned out last week (three and a half pounds, planted January 14, 'Maris Bard'). As her ladyship was in Sussex at the time they were sent there, with other vegetables such as ordinary potatoes, carrots, beetroots, parsnips, bulb onions, salad onions, leeks, cabbage, asparagus, sprouting broccoli, lettuce, rhubarb, mint, parsley, thyme, sage and chives, neatly packed in a box with a few pot plants.

In the vegetable wash room the delivery being prepared for the Hall today consists of: bundles of asparagus, trimmed, graded into thick and thin and wrapped in white paper skirts, a few spring cabbages, some white sprouting broccoli, some lettuces and some spring onions. Parsnips and carrots from the store are being scrubbed under the cold tap. Onions are having to be bought, as 10 per cent were lost in the store during the winter and now there are not enough.

The fruit room is almost empty except for a few yellow, but still good, 'Bramleys' and 'Christmas Pippins'. Old gardening books tell of certain varieties of apple lasting till May, or even longer (Evelyn mentions the 'Gold Doucet', the 'Pepins' and an apple that was meant to last two years, the 'Deux-ans'). Doug's fruit room will certainly be empty by the end of the month. Evelyn also lists apples which ripen in June, thus providing seventeenth-century gardeners with apples all the year round. Doug's first apples, his 'Worcester Pearmains' and 'Yellow Codlings', will not ripen before August, but true to tradition, as soon as the fruit room is empty it will be thoroughly cleaned and scrubbed, ready for the new season.

The fruit room here is built like the mushroom shed with 18-inch-thick brick walls, whitewashed inside. There are ventilators at the top and bottom of these walls but no windows. The roof is of slate with two more shuttered ventilators in it. Inside, the roof is lined with tongue-and-grooved wood, providing enough space for good insulation. There are deep shelves either side of a central gangway, made of slatted oak. The front two-thirds of each shelf is on brass runners so that it can be completely taken out to make the back third of the shelf (which remains fixed in place) more accessible. The shelves have been tailor-made for each row;

asparagus & new potatoes
('Duke of York')

to make sure they are returned to their proper places each one has a roman numeral carved on its front face. (A similar system of numbering is sometimes seen on cold frame lights.) There are ten bays, each with four shelves in it. The grape bottles were fitted along the fronts of special shelves with retaining bars to keep them in place.

This fruit room is not heated but even in the bitterest weather it has always been frost-free. It answers perfectly to the requirements of a fruit room described by James Anderson in his *New Practical Gardener*, a book that was published towards the end of the nineteenth century. He wrote, 'The three important points for conservers of fruit to study are an exclusion from air-currents, the maintaining of a low temperature in spring and summer, and the exclusion of a glare of light. Very little artificial warmth is necessary even in the coldest winters; fire heat has a desiccating tendency upon fruit, ripe or unripe.' In short, he says, a fruit room should be sunless, as free from damp as possible, and capable of excluding the extremes of heat and cold. The shelves should be of hard wood rather than pine 'which communicates an unpleasant flavour to the fruit'. He also recommends fixing canvas or holland blinds on rollers 'to be let down in front of the shelves for the exclusion of dust, cold, or air'. (This is a refinement which the fruit room at Cottesbrooke does not have.)

Out of doors the peach tree on the wall in the Middle Garden shows sign of leaf-curl and looks wretched, but the apricot fruit is setting and so are some of the cherries, though the morello is yet to flower. The outdoor early potatoes are up, showing small furry leaves, but there is no sign so far of any growth along the rows of main-crop potatoes. Eight rows of onion sets ('Sturon' and 'Fenlander') and six rows of onion seedlings ('Rhinesburger') have been planted and in a seed-bed there are labels showing that borecole, two varieties of cauliflower, sweet Williams and beetroot were sown last Friday.

There are a few signs of summer. Along the side of the path leading to Doug's house, a palisade of tall poles has been erected for the sweet peas to climb up. These were planted out three weeks ago, leaving an empty space in the vinery for the first time in many months. The gladioli, saved as corms last October, have been planted in the bed in front of the old disused greenhouse. In the other Top Garden greenhouse over-wintered standard fuchsias are ready to be planted out in the Hall gardens. The border running down the length of the frame yard under the almshouse garden wall is ready for the early chrysanthemums. The Dutch irises in the cold frames have had their lights taken off. The mats and coverings from the cold frames have been put in the boilerhouse to dry off. There is still ground frost at night, but the coverings are not needed now.

All the vegetable seedlings and bedding plants raised in the propagation house or heated frames have either been hardened off and planted out or are still in cold frames.

Weeding is the biggest chore out of doors. The outdoor irises, herb bed, rhubarb and strawberries have all been weeded. The weeding, done mainly by Sid, John and Teresa, accentuates the contrast between the thin lines of seedlings and the freshly hoed broader strips of brown earth. Spinach, peas, carrots, Texsel greens, swedes, spring onions, beetroot, broad beans and parsnips have all come up. The peas have been staked with leafy bamboo canes trimmed from the Wild Garden up at the Hall.

The propagation house is now filled with cucumbers and melons from end to end. Ken and Doug are kept busy here, pinching out the stray vines, taping the leaders to supporting wires and pollinating the female flowers with the pistils of the male flowers.

Joy is still in the potting shed, sitting on her new stool and potting up seedlings of *Acer palmatum*. After a visit to a large commercial nursery in Norfolk, where five- and six-year-old acers are sold for £20 each, Doug knows the value of raising his own trees from seed. He is perfectly happy working in these gardens but should this job ever come to an end, he would like to run a commercial garden. The propagation and planting of trees and shrubs is one of his favourite departments of gardening. He shows me the shoots on a large, old azalea which would make good cuttings. 'The interesting thing', he says, looking at another, younger azalea, 'is that there are just as many good shoots on this smaller, but more vigorous plant.' He makes a very good teacher and did indeed at one point in his career have such a post, as the gardening instructor in an open prison.

Halfway through the afternoon Doug is visited by an itinerant rat-catcher who travels about the country with a mobile shop. Doug buys two pairs of heavy gloves, a bucket, a brush, a pine broom handle for the brush and an ash hoe handle. The hoe handle, he points out, has a nice

Red currants in blossom

waist at the top to hold on to. Other wares on offer (I quote from the rat-catcher's leaflet) are 'Traps and snares; dog food; Mebenret and Gapex; poisons, shirts and socks; nails and staples; water-proofs; drinkers, rings and bits; knives and hardware'.

At the far end of the potting shed Jess, wearing his usual dark-blue boiler suit, has finished mending and painting the lantern cloches and is busy with a ledger in which he has listed all his carnation cuttings. The carnation house, 18 feet wide and 30 feet long, is his responsibility; he says it can take 500 full-sized carnation pots. His other duty, performed every Friday, is the feeding of all the pot plants in all the hothouses. He uses liquid feed, either Phostrogen or Vitax, which is dispensed in the right proportion of feed to water through a special drum (a Cameron diluter) to which a watering hose can be attached. The whole job takes him five hours, but he has been gardening long enough to remember giving plants his own, non-proprietary mixture (a liquid manure made by soaking a bag of soot and sheep dung in a barrel of rainwater) which contained all the necessary chemicals (animal, vegetable and mineral) for good plant growth.

Until the discovery, in the mid-nineteenth century by Justus von Leibig, that plants depend on three main elements (nitrogen, phosphorus and potassium) for growth, scientists and chemists had been of little help to gardeners on the subject of plant nutrition. Loudon, writing in 1830, observed that 'much has been written on soils, and till lately, to very little purpose.' He mentions 'the Roman authors on husbandry' and 'copious philosophical dis-courses on soils by Bacon, Evelyn, Bradley and others', but adds 'in no department of cultivation was ever so much written of which so little use could be made by practical men.' His own contributions on fertilisers and manures are drawn mainly from Sir Humphry Davy's *Lectures on Agricultural Chemistry*, in the edition of 1821. His list of suitable animal and vegetable manures for the soil is remarkably similar to that of the ancient Romans. Loudon recommends: green crop manures including pond weeds and the parings of hedges and ditches; rape cake, malt dust, the water in which flax and hemp have been retted; seaweeds (used fresh); dry straw ploughed in immediately after the crops had been harvested; wood-ashes; animal manures, animal carcases and fish; blubber mixed with clay or sand; bones ground to dust and bone shavings; horn, hair, woollen rags and feathers; refuse from the workings of curriers, furriers, tanyards and glue makers; blood and 'the scum taken from the boilers of the sugar bakers' (who used bullocks' blood to refine their sugar); corals, corallines and sponges; urine (animal and human); bird dung, particularly guano; nightsoil

Ken in the potting shed, with décor for the Hall

mixed with quicklime (this was sold in London in cakes under the name of 'Clarkes desiccated compost'); street and road dung and the sweepings of horses, and lastly, soot 'thrown into the ground with the seed'.

In the eighteenth and early nineteenth centuries hothouse plants were fed quite simply with liquid manures made either by 'steeping the dung of sheep or pigeons in a quantity of water until it becomes highly impregnated with it' (MacIntosh 1828) or with more exciting mixtures such as this one, for orange trees: the gardener 'after the fruit is set, waters with water, in which, at the rate of three barrows of fresh cow-dung, without litter, two barrows of fresh sheep's droppings, and two pecks of quicklime have been added to every hogshead; when used, the water is about the consistence of cream'. (*Horticultural Transactions*, v, 310)

The last job of the day is to assemble the pot plants for the Hall. Her ladyship returns from Sussex tomorrow which means that a completely new décor will have to be installed. The potting shed bench is swept down and cleared. It is 24 feet long, and lit by a window running from end to end. Doug sends Ken, John, Teresa and Jess from one house to another with trolleys and cardboard boxes, to fetch a total of eighty-five pot plants which will be assembled on the potting shed bench, taking up the whole of it.

apple blossom by the polytunnel

There are: five varieties of regal pelargonium, a box of begonias (variety 'President Carnot') and one box each of lemon-scented geraniums, ivy-leaved geraniums and gold-leaved geraniums. The bench is like a gigantic window-box, a mass of pink, red and purple. For cut flowers there are carnations, geraniums, arum lilies and, 'as a conversation piece', anigozanthus, a tall furry green flower from Australia, popularly known as kangaroo paws.

Hugh takes a last glum look at the orchard. Nothing has altered since this morning; it is cold, green and unflowering. Instead he turns his attention to the old apple trees beside the poly tunnel. They at least have begun to blossom, possibly because the Middle Garden is more sheltered than the orchard, which slopes downwards towards the north and the frost-pocket created by the lake.

Next week Doug will concentrate on getting the gardens into tip-top condition for the Open Day on May 26, a Bank Holiday.

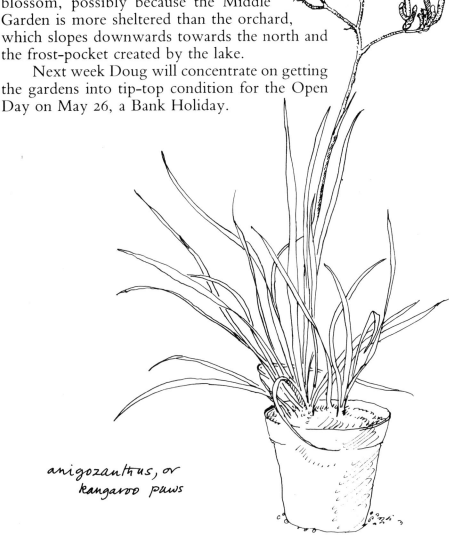

anigozanthus, or kangaroo paws

JUNE

Ninth visit Monday, 10 June 1985

There is now full leaf on all the trees. The early morning sun accentuates the contours of the old ridge and furrow fields which lie on either side of the gated road leading to Cottesbrooke. In the meadows cattle graze in knee-high grass. In the park the ewes, which looked like dumpy grey bundles last time we came, are thin-necked and white against their rich, dark-green pasture – they have just been shorn; they have also been parted from their lambs and the air is full of bleating. It looks as if summer is here at last, but most of the weather since our last visit has been appalling, as I can see from Doug's journal.

On the Open Day on May 26 it rained continuously; in spite of this there were 109 visitors and £120 was made for the Nurses' Benevolent Fund. (This year the fund was boosted by selling four dozen lettuces at 20p each and five dozen pot plants at 50p each.) Doug's journal then records that although the last few days of May and the first few days of June brought very warm, dry sunny weather it quickly deteriorated into thunderstorms, to be followed by dull, humid weather with drizzly rain. Finally at the end of the first week of June, on the Thursday and Friday, it rained heavily and continuously for thirty-six hours.

This has had no adverse effect on the gardens so far; if anything it has saved the gardeners the chore of watering. The quarters in the Middle Garden are filling up; rows of spinach, swede and radish which were narrow lines three weeks ago are now broad stripes, almost touching. Dwarf beans have been planted out, but over the weekend a pheasant or partridge, or both, has been all down the rows, tweaking off the tops. The same thing has happened to a row of broccoli in the Top Garden. Although Doug is a keen observer of birds, and has recently been most distressed to find that Rodney, his cat, has killed a wren that had almost become a pet in the vinery, he is furious about these game-birds. 'Stupid things, you have to frighten them to make them fly and even then they don't have the sense to avoid being shot.' He has a plan to shoot them himself. Thinking that this is somewhat unsporting, I suggest putting plastic carrier bags on string tied to tall canes, having found that this works very well in my own garden in Hampshire. His humming strands of plastic tape are still in place, wailing constantly like lost souls, but the birds have obviously become accustomed to the sound. We find six carrier bags printed with the names of Fisons and Tesco and arrange them along the bean rows. John, who is now wearing contact lenses instead of his usual spectacles, is despatched to Doug's office to find a reel of Seedling Protection Thread, thick black cotton which he will arrange along the bean rows as well. He looks far less short-sighted without his specs.

Seedlings that have not been attacked by birds are doing very

John & Ken hoeing, Top Garden

well. The sweetcorn is about nine inches high (there are 420 plants according to Doug's journal); the onions of all varieties are well forward; outdoor lettuces by the poly tunnel are nearly fully grown. Celeriac has been planted out and Florence fennel sown; both of these are fairly unusual vegetables, especially for a cook who, I suspect, is required to be fairly conservative and unadventurous, sticking to tried and tested family recipes and not demanding anything too outlandish from the kitchen gardens. However, Doug, as a good head gardener should be, is always interested in trying something new; when I offer him a packet of the white carrot seed which I bought on a recent visit to France, he jumps at it.

All of Jess's eleven lantern cloches are in use, each protecting a young courgette seedling. A deep hole was dug for each plant the same size as the cloche, then filled with well-rotted manure and capped with a little mound of earth. The courgette seedlings were then planted on top and the cloches placed over them. It is John's responsibility to ventilate the cloches if necessary by moving the lids aside or even taking them off altogether; he must also make sure they are replaced at night. By the end of the month the plants should be large enough and the weather warm enough for the cloches to be taken off completely. Trenches have also been dug, manured and planted with celery; one row of 'Giant White', one of 'Giant Pink', one of 'Fenlander'; sixty plants to a row. They will be earthed up later in the summer and should be ready in late October, lasting till January. It remains to be seen if the part of the garden chosen for this year's crop, by the bungalow, is less slug-ridden than the part chosen last year, by the poly tunnel. Doug says an old garden is always full of slugs. The new patch had been occupied by nursery trees for the past few years and was infested, not with slugs, but with couch grass. This was laboriously dug out by Sid at the end of May to prepare the ground for celery and runner bean trenches. Four varieties of runner beans have already been sown in trays and are hardened off, ready for planting: 'Achievement', 'Polestar', 'Butler' and 'Streamline' are their names, lovely names that seem to me to be more suitable for steam engines or racing yachts. I am still puzzling over the question of how plant-breeders arrive at names for different varieties of quite ordinary plants; there are obvious reasons for calling a winter cauliflower 'Snowcap', or a potato 'McKinlay's Pride', but how does a melon become 'Romeo' or a lettuce 'Nabucco'?

The fruit cage, planted with black, red and white currants, gooseberries, raspberries and loganberries, has had its top net replaced. This was done by all seven gardeners working in a line inside the cage – Ken, Joy, John, Sid, Teresa, Jess and Doug, unrolling the net from one side to another, their arms above their heads. Fresh straw has been laid under the strawberries in one of the borders; their netting goes on tomorrow.

In the tunnel the early potatoes are now cropping; Teresa is in here pulling radishes both red and white as well as spring onions and the first young carrots. She has picked peas, broad beans and strawberries too. Aubergines and Chinese gooseberries have been planted here since our last visit. There are also tomatoes, some in pots, others in the ground. The latter look sickly – the ground was manured before they were planted and the straw in it must have come from a crop that had been treated with weedkiller. Doug hopes they'll pull through, but this is a hazard of modern gardening.

Teresa washes the carrots, radishes and spring onions and ties

Teresa hoeing onions in the Top Garden

radishes and spring onions

them in small bundles with raffia. She also trims and washes asparagus, then wraps each bunch in a paper skirt, fastening it with a rubber band. The first cucumbers are ready in the propagation house, which is now referred to as the melon house. They drip from the roof like green stalactites. The melon vines and their leaves almost obliterate the sky; the melons hang in nylon nets like hard green breasts – none is ripe yet.

All the lights have been taken off the cold frames; lettuces growing here are now ready for eating. They share the frames with boxes of wallflowers for next year's bedding, the seed is just showing through. The heated frames have been painted with 'Summer Cloud'; all the glasshouses except the peach houses, melon house and vinery, which need maximum sun, are shaded inside with polythene sheeting. In the orchid or stove house (which is kept at a steady 60° to 70°F) many of the seeds sown by Doug in January and February are now handsome pot plants in flower. Here is a mass of pink-flowered echevarias and bright orange *Asclepia curassavica* (sown on January 28); John, who has responsibility for this house, calls it milkweed. Here too are pink climbing foxgloves (*Maurandia barclaiana*) arranged in spirals; white, blue and purple achimenes or hot-water plants (repotted on January 14, and grown from tubercles); *Tweedia caerulia* and *Gesneria cardinalis* mixed, both sown on February 4 and now making a splash of delicate blue and bright red. The *Begonia sutherlandii*, of all these exotic plants, strikes me as most unusual with its almost black leaves and sprays of small orange flowers.

With so many blooms, *primeurs* and first fruits now ready I begin to see the reason for all the hard work done by the gardeners earlier in the year. The first nectarine was picked four days after our last visit in May, on the 19th, an event that Doug relates as nonchalantly as if it had been the first of his cabbages. Thirteen more were picked and sent to the house before the end of the month, finishing the crop from the earliest tree which is only a young one. Hydrangeas and fuchsias occupy the beds of the peach house at the warmest end of this range, but the beds beneath the vines and the beds in the fig and peach house at the cooler end are now quite empty; the clivias and arum lilies that occupied that space are lined up outside and will stay here till September, resting.

The arums have been flowering since Christmas. There are twelve of them; each flowered once a week. The fig leaves have grown so large they form a complete canopy over their curved trellis. Grapes droop in long, pale-green bunches from the vinery roof; the earliest peach tree ('Hale's Early') is covered with small pink and gold pompoms. Like its blossom, the fruit looks so pretty and ornamental it is difficult to believe that it is real; the tree appears to be decorated with the flock-covered glass balls that are sold for Christmas trees; they might even be peaches made of velvet, or marzipan. Hugh and I are admiring this sight with Doug and Ken, when both of them tilt back their heads and sniff. 'Smell of peaches!' cries Doug. Hugh and I are mystified by their excitement. Ken feels about in the tree very gently. He cups his hand

'Peregrine' peaches, nearly ripe

PEACH PEREGRINE

beneath three fruit in turn, lifts each one until its stem parts from the branch and hands them to Doug. If a peach house smells of peaches, it means they're ripe. These are the first of the year. Doug takes them to his office and opens the green-painted cupboard which occupies the whole of the back wall. The contents might almost belong to a stationer's shop. Here he keeps what are described by his suppliers as 'gardeners' sundries': reams of pink, green and white tissue papers, balls of string, elastic bands, assorted sizes of cardboard boxes and plastic punnets, tapes, staplers and hormone rooting powders. He chooses a white cardboard box just big enough for the two largest peaches, nestles them in white tissue paper and shares the third peach, which is not very big, with me. I have read somewhere of a pear having a flood of 'sprightly juice'. This is what comes to my mind as I bite into that peach. It has, once peeled, the whitest flesh, with a pale-green tinge just beneath the skin.

Outside, on the other side of the frame yard, Jess has a couple of lines stretched along the length of the wide gravel path that runs behind the greenhouses. He knocks posts in at intervals and stretches wires between them. Below the wires he has two rows, each one contains 194 winter-flowering chrysanthemums, in pots. The plants are only a few inches high at present, but each is provided with a five-foot cane to support it when it is fully grown. Jess ties the canes to the wires. The rows now look like two lines of soldiers standing very straight. The chrysanthemums will be disbudded as they grow. They will be moved into the vinery at the end of September, where they will flower until January.

Tomorrow is Tuesday, not the usual day for a full replenishment of all the planters and jardinières up at the Hall, but her ladyship is returning from a fortnight in Scotland and there has been no décor during her absence. Ken and Doug assemble what they need in the afternoon so that it will be ready for them to pack into the van early next morning. Their conversation reflects the process by which Doug decides on his décor. We are standing in the lower peach house looking at the pots of hydrangeas.

Doug: 'Can you find a couple of Formosa fern, Ken, and a couple

pink hydrangeas,
décor for the Hall

of coleus? . . . We haven't talked about hydrangeas have we?' No answer. 'She wants two in the drawing room, two in the dining room, two in the pine room . . .' (This is another, pine-panelled drawing room.)

Ken: 'What about cut flowers?'

Doug: 'No cut flowers till Thursday or Friday.' Doug is musing. Ken suggests helpfully: 'There's some begonias in the bottom frame . . . and what about the orangey-flowered doings?'

Doug: 'The *sutherlandii*? Yes, some of them and look at the fuchsias in the cold frame. We'll use a hotch potch for the coffin.' (This is a coffin-shaped planter standing on barley-sugar-shaped legs.) 'Check out the "Lavender Slams".' (These are regal pelargoniums, and a variation of the bright-red 'Grand Slam'.) 'And let's have two lots of abutilons . . .'

This break in the routine for the décor was expected. The trouble comes when the break is unexpected. Everything is ready with nowhere to go. 'It's like a goods train when the engine stops. All the trucks go shunting into one another', says Doug.

In the late afternoon sun even the poly tunnel looks pretty. Its skin is stretched tightly over its ribs, reflecting clear blue sky, lush green growth, pink brick walls and rich brown earth. We are waiting for the sun to move round to the morello cherry on the north wall behind the herb bed. The herb bed looks good. In it Doug grows all the herbs a cook could need – parsley and mint of

a view of the Hall, south front, taken from the Lake

course (both are available all the year round, coming from the poly tunnel in winter and from outdoors in the summer), chives (which are at the moment flowering prolifically), thyme (in great bushy cushions), sage, caraway, marjoram, fennel, basil, tarragon, chervil, rosemary and horseradish. The morello cherry is in flower and is a mass of white blossom. The gages on the west wall look good too; they were not caught by frost and are already forming fruit. The apples in the orchard are poor, not because of the frost but because most of the trees are old and have canker.

We are still waiting at 7 o'clock for the sun to hit the morello. Ken and John have been watering, but now it's time for them to lock up. As if to nudge us on our way the sun falls below the trees between us and the churchyard before it reaches the cherry. John closes his lantern cloches and walks with us to our car, which is parked between his house and the back of the potting shed. He watches us packing up the camera gear and says rather wistfully that the nearest he's ever been to London is Hampton Court, on a school outing. 'What has he been missing?' we ask ourselves as we drive, without much enthusiasm, back in that direction.

Tenth visit Friday, 28 June 1985

Activity in the gardens and hothouses has increased so much that we need to make two visits in June to keep up with everything.

In order to watch the gardeners arranging their interior décor we leave London at 5.30 am. We stop for an over-long breakfast on the motorway and finish the journey recklessly, at well over the speed limit. We get to the gardens on the dot of half past seven, still enmeshed in the nervous excitement of driving fast, which rapidly untangles as we watch Doug, Joy and Ken calmly finish packing the van with some ninety pot plants that were selected the day before and stored overnight in the potting shed. There are dark pink echevarias, tall orange milkweeds, small pink begonias and yellowy-green-leaved coleus. This mixture of colours, shapes and various heights looks most inharmonious at present, jammed as it is into an assortment of cardboard boxes. Moreover, there is a little hitch; instead of standing bolt upright the echevarias are all leaning one way, like bent bows. They have grown like this after moving from the stove house to the cold frames. Joy struggles to re-pot them so that they will stand up straight, but to no avail. With the hope that they can, nevertheless, be fitted into the arrangements on the spot they are taken along just as they are.

Driving in convoy behind the van we press through a herd of cows standing on the little bridge beyond the main lodge gates and sweep through the park, up to the front steps of the Hall.

Chives flowering in the herb bed

Doug lays a spotless path of sacking drugget across the Hall floor, carries in his new supplies and, with Ken and Joy, starts to dismantle the planters and jardinières, putting the pot plants that formed last week's display in the boxes left empty by this week's delivery. Out go the white begonias in the planters on either side of the door: in go the twenty-four new pots of striped impatiens. Ken raises them to the proper height in their deep, lead-lined oval mahogany tubs by standing them on empty, reversed pots. They are raked up at the back, so that the flowers look like hundreds of little faces peering out from two grandstands.

Next, fourteen begonias with enormous, blood-red flowers are arranged in a neat pyramid in a huge wooden urn at the foot of the stairs and then, in the south-facing, pine-panelled drawing room with its beautiful view of the distant steeple far away across the park, the team remove last week's achimenes and hydrangeas and get to grips with this week's echevarias and milkweed. These make a fine combination of pink and orange with the plain, unpainted panelling behind them, but the echevarias are still hopelessly bowed, ruining the effect. Ken and Doug kneel before the planter, hats off, sleeves rolled up. Joy stands critically behind them. They look like the figures in a panel from a Florentine altarpiece, but Doug swears discreetly and the echevarias are returned to their cardboard box to go back to the gardens. (They can be used as cut flowers later, as they smell so sweet.) Their place is taken by the pale-pink begonias, which are shorter than the echevarias and the cause of a considerable amount of re-arrangement. A dozen pots are accounted for here.

Next comes the planter on the lower staircase. This is the one called 'the coffin' on account of its shape; it's a long, pale box on twisted barley-sugar legs, with a high ornate mirror behind it. It will take eighteen to twenty pots. Here we have more milkweed, which is tall and goes at the back, more pink begonias, which are short and arranged in front, and the yellow-green coleus, which goes in at each end. This planter is easy; for some reason, according to Doug, it's always easy.

Lastly there are the jardinières, two huge Chinese pots on the massive hall table; each one can hold up to nine plants. They are filled with blue hydrangeas and more begonias. The house is busy on this floor; above it there is silence. Everyone up there is still sleeping, or just waking. I hear a noise like bathwater running out, continuously, but the noise is not from the drainpipes – it comes from the fountain in one of the garden pools just outside the house. On this floor, the *piano nobile*, there are fine views of the pleasure gardens. To the south-west the windows overlook Doug's chequerboard parterre of pink geraniums and blue lobelia in the Dutch garden. Beyond it stretches the long herbaceous border walk. To the south-east, on the front terrace, an outside gardener is watering urns filled with more geraniums, using water from a garden engine. Another mows the lawn beyond the terrace. One Friesian cow stands on the far side of the ha-ha and a flock of sheep moves across the middle distance in front of the lake, like sheep in a Claude landscape.

Not long after we arrived every clock in the house started chiming, each in its own well-ordered and well-oiled fashion; it was eight o'clock. Now it is about half-past.

At nine all the clocks strike again; the pot plant arrangements are finished. The butler appears with the post and the newspapers. A smell of toast and baking scones comes with him from the kitchen. It's time for us to go back to Doug's house for coffee, checking the vegetable supply before we leave. Today he will send to the cook:

new potatoes	*spinach*	*lettuce*
cauliflowers	*broad beans*	*baby carrots*
spring cabbage	*French beans (hothouse)*	*baby beetroots*
cucumbers (hothouse)	*Japanese onions*	*salad onions*
outdoor strawberries		
peaches (hothouse)		

The first two tomatoes of the season have already been sent, but not, as yet, any melons. On his return to the gardens Doug checks the melon house, finds that one is actually ripe and calls everyone within reach for a sniff of it. It is a 'Blenheim Orange', dark yellow but almost covered with a raised network of paler yellow lines. Ken, Joy and Teresa, summoned from the task of returning the used pot plants to the frames outside the vinery, sniff it, smiling with pride and pleasure. I sniff it; the scent of all the fruit and flowers in the world seems to come from it. It has to be taken at once to the Hall, on a separate, special journey.

Although it is only eighteen days since we were here last, there has been progress and growth everywhere. The sweet peas, retarded by the poor weather, are starting to flower; the poles are in place for the runner beans; the outdoor French beans are through; the first early outdoor potatoes ('Dunluce') are being dug up by Teresa. In the poly tunnel the early peas and lettuces have all gone, but the newly planted capsicums, aubergines, Chinese gooseberries, 'Ogen' melons and cucumbers are flourishing; the ailing tomatoes look better; a row of beetroot is through; the self-blanching celery is nearly ready; the strawberries are finished

summer veg. in the stone sink

and the broad beans nearly so.

Ken will take over as dutyman this evening. Doug walks the dutyman, whoever it may be, round the gardens every Friday afternoon, showing him where to water and where not to, what to ventilate and how much, what to keep closed, which houses or frames to open up if it's warm and which to shut down if it's cold. The boilers are now turned off until September. 'Keep the peachhouse doors shut at all times', he warns, 'or the blackbirds will fly in.'

As we walk through the Top Garden Doug ruffles the leaves of two long rows of kohlrabi and turnips. The largest roots in both lines are just the size of golf balls, Doug would have sent some of them to the Hall this morning, if he'd known they were ready. I see now why some of the vegetables are planted here on such a huge scale; they are eaten long before they reach full size, when they are really tiny. The wet weather has relieved the gardeners of the job of outside watering; the rain has actually caused the peas and broad beans to outgrow their supporting sticks and canes by feet, rather than inches. The weeds have grown at a similar rate, giving Doug another problem; if this was a normal Friday he would concentrate on planting out his brassicas and potting up the 300 cyclamen corms that arrived this morning, but Sunday is the second Open Day this year and everyone (except Jess who is off sick) must hoe and weed so that the place looks spick and span. The Gardens, both here and up at the Hall, are opened to the public three times a year, in May, June and September, in order to raise funds for charity. These occasions are advertised locally and anything up to 500 people can be expected, especially if, as happened once last year, the event is mentioned on local radio. Doug's feelings about the visitors to Open Days are a mixture of pride and anxiety, hence his concern with the weeding. 'If there's one weed to be seen, no matter how many we've removed, someone will spot it.'

With Mac, John, Sid and Teresa bent over their hoes, Doug takes on the responsibility, once Ken has been walked round the gardens, of planting out leeks, another urgent job. The leeks are labelled 'Giant Winter'; they were sown on March 29 and pricked out, he says, at the end of April. The bed they are going into is the bed that has been used for leeks for the past sixteen years. He plants them in holes that he makes with a steel-tipped dibber, without trimming their tops or tails, nine inches apart in rows twelve inches apart. There are 68 rows, 12 leeks to a row, making 816 leeks in all. This is not the sort of job Doug normally does, but with one gardener sick he has to help the others. While he works he tells me a bit about how he learned his craft; he worked at eight different places in all before coming here, starting in the Municipal Parks Department in his home-town, Stoke-on-Trent, progressing to instructor in the prison gardens and allotments at Ley Hill and penultimately working as gardens manager at Trentham Park, where the estate with its grand Italian gardens had been opened up as a country park. This progress from place to place is called 'moving on' in the gardening world; its apparent restlessness is due to the difficulty of being promoted or learning more about other branches of gardening by staying in the same place. Unless the gardener above you in the hierarchy either moves on himself, is given the sack, retires or dies, a gardener may remain an under-gardener all his life. By moving from one kind of gardening job to another Doug learnt everything he needed to know for his present post – greenhouse work, ornamental garden work, park work and kitchen garden work – without ever being in private service before.

Loudon, in his *Encyclopaedia of Gardening*, describes the progression of a gardener through the ranks, early in the nineteenth century. The restlessness has a remarkable similarity to Doug's career, 150 years later on. No doubt if there had been enough eminent 'private gardens' left, of the old-fashioned kind, in which he could have learnt what he needed to know he would have worked in them, rather than in a country park or an open prison. In Loudon's time the gardener began work (unless he wished to be no more than a garden-labourer) as an apprentice to a master-gardener. Apprenticeship usually lasted three years or longer if the boy was under 16 but it could not continue after he was 21. 'The, period of apprenticeship being finished, that of journeyman commences, and continues, or ought to continue till the man is at least twenty-five years of age. During this period, he ought not to remain above one year in any one situation; thus, supposing he has completed his apprenticeship in a private garden at the age of twenty-one, and that his ultimate object is to become a head-gardener, he ought first to engage himself a year in a public botanic garden; the next year in a public nursery; that following he should again enter a private garden, and continue making yearly changes in the most eminent of this class of gardens, till he meets with a

Sid weeding the asparagus beds

Teresa picking peas in the poly tunnel

situation as head-gardener . . .' The journeyman of longest standing would be appointed foreman over other journeymen in gardens where there were three or more journeymen. This, in Loudon's day, 'conferred a certain degree of rank for the time being, but none afterwards.' The next move up the scale was to 'attain the *situation* of a master-gardener'. This 'situation' entailed appointment to 'the management of a garden even if he has no laborer, apprentice or journeyman under him'. The *rank* of master-gardener (the equivalent today of a gardens manager) was reached after one year in such a situation. Loudon's head-gardener or upper gardener was a master with apprentices or journeymen employed under him.

The present arrangement in the kitchen gardens at Cottesbrooke finds Sid acting as garden labourer, Joy, John and Teresa as trainee gardeners, Jess as propagator and Ken as chargehand, which is one step below foreman. Modern grades begin with garden labourer, progress to trainee gardener (school-leavers and apprentices are included in this group) and continue with gardener, craftsman I, craftsman II (depending on the number of approved qualifications), propagator, chargehand (in charge of a section of a department), foreman (responsible for a whole department), finally ending with head gardener. None of Doug's kitchen garden staff has actually had any formal gardening education, but he says that Jess, having worked as a propagator in a commercial nursery before coming here is one of the élite of the gardening trade. 'Knifemen', as propagators are also known, are in a class of their own, according to Doug. They earn their title by learning the proper way to take cuttings, prune, bud and graft. These crafts are ancient; they were written about at length in the garden manuals of the Greeks and Romans and have been written about, at length, in gardening manuals ever since. Stephen Switzer, an eighteenth-century gardener, seedsman, garden-designer and author of several books on gardens, was well aware of the risks attached to this branch of gardening. He had this to say on the subject of the knife in a 'Proemical Discourse concerning Pruning of Fruit-Trees' (*The Practical Fruit-Gardener*, 1724): 'There is not (it may be with much Truth affirmed) in the whole Compass of the Art of Gardening, any Point that is more curious and useful than the regular Conduct of the Knife in the Pruning of Fruit-Trees, neither is there any Part of Gardening more pretended to, nor really less understood than it is: For though the Rules are not many, nor the Difficulties great, yet every one that can but handle the Knife a little, is so well pleas'd with it, that he seldom takes Pains enough to improve in his Art, but to prune on by rote . . .'

Cucumbers, netting and string in the wash room

The weeding done, each gardener makes sure the house for which he or she has special responsibility is ready for the Open Day, which is in aid of the Gardeners' Benevolent Fund this time. John checks the lean-to in the Top Garden and the stove house, Ken sees to the vinery range, Teresa re-arranges all the pot plants (mainly begonias and *Primula obconicas*) in her palm house, Doug looks at Jess's carnation house and his own melon house. Joy has fed and watered all the frames. I note that in the Top Gardens greenhouse there is space for the last planting of cucumbers. The earliest cucumbers (the ones growing in the melon house) are nearly finished. They began fruiting on May 18 and are now superseded by those in the poly tunnel. With the cucumbers in the top greenhouse to come, the gardens will be able to keep up their supply until November. The same succession is kept up with the tomatoes, the second crop is ready now in the top house; the first crop came from the vinery and the third crop will come from the tunnel.

There is one more thing for Doug to see to before he can go home; the Open Day notices for directing the public must be taken out of the box shed, cleaned and put ready for collection and placing by the outside gardeners. We leave him surrounded by a little grove of white posts topped by signboards with arrows. They say 'Wild Garden', 'Car Park', 'Pool Garden', 'Dutch Garden', 'Teas', 'Ladies', 'Gents' and 'Kitchen Garden'.

signboards for Open Day

JULY

Eleventh visit Tuesday, 16 July 1985

After one of the coldest, wettest midsummer months on record, July began with a little heat-wave. On Tuesday 2 July Doug wrote in his journal: 'Fine, warm and dry! Summer at last?' On Thursday 4 July it was '80°F. in the shade at 12.30pm'. This was hotter than the day before, which had been the warmest day so far, but yesterday, July 15, it 'Started to rain 6.30pm' and when we arrived today it was still raining.

The soft fruits, nevertheless, are ripening in profusion. The chief reason for this visit is to keep up with the picking of countless figs, black, white and red currants, gooseberries, raspberries, peaches and strawberries. Those that are not eaten fresh will be bottled, canned, frozen or made into jam. Four hundred peaches have been bottled already, 240 having been picked for bottling in one day. Two hundred came off one tree; 600 or 700 have already been picked and there are still more to come. Some are quite small, but they taste delicious. Hugh and I begin the day with one each, carefully peeling off the furry skin, biting into the greenish-white flesh. They are not 99 per cent but 100 per cent juice; it pours down our chins as we bite.

The first figs were picked on July 1. When they are nearly ready their unripe green skin turns brownish. Doug waits for a small split to appear in each fruit before he picks it. This is the surest sign of a ripe fig. A few of their own leaves are sent with them to decorate the dish in which they will be served, as the butler arranges all the fruit for the table. At some grand houses, even in the quite recent past, I know that the head gardener always had this job; the butler would send salvers and dishes to the gardens, to minimise disturbance of the fruit. I sense that Doug would quite like that to be the custom here; he can hardly

figs arranged on a plate

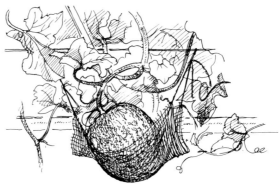

'Emerald Gem' in
a safety net

bear to think of the bruising that would occur if his peaches or figs
were clumsily handled, or the spoiling of the bloom if they were
too often picked up and put down. He is not at all surprised when I
tell him that Victorian and Edwardian gardeners were supposed to
pick peaches, nectarines and figs in white cotton gloves. Loudon
describes a peach-gathering implement for picking fruit that is out
of reach. It is 'a tin funnel or inverted hollow cone, [elsewhere he
says this should be lined with velvet] fixed on the end of a rod or
handle at an obtuse angle, the funnel is first introduced under each
fruit, and then gently raised or moved sideways; if ripe, the fruit
will fall into the funnel.' This is one contrivance that the Cottesbrooke gardeners can do without. Instead, their greenhouse
ladders have two projecting arms about fifteen inches long fixed to
the tops and backs of the side supports. This keeps the top of the
ladder away from the wall and allows a person to pick peaches or
nectarines without any fear of squashing the fruit with the ladder.

In the melon house there has been a problem; the fruit keeps
splitting as it ripens, making it too unsightly to send to the house.
Doug thinks the solution is to water less, but more often. The roof
of the melon house is full of melons, each one is provided with a
little safety net of green nylon as soon as it reaches a decent size, to
take the weight off the vine. There are three kinds, all designed to
ripen in succession. First are the yellow-netted 'Blenheim
Orange', next will come the little dark green 'Emerald Gem' and
lastly, the blotchily striped 'Tiger'.

Inside the fruit cage John and Teresa are picking a new variety
of red currant, 'Janker van Tets'. This is Doug's favourite. The
fruit is huge, hanging like bunches of miniature red grapes. John
and Teresa pick fruit every morning now. When the fruit cage is
done they crawl on all fours under the bright-blue netting on the

Sweet peas by the almshouse wall

strawberry beds; the variety being picked at the moment is 'Bogota'. It yields huge berries; they picked one berry last week weighing 2¾ ounces. Yesterday they picked 31 pounds of straw-berries; the week before that they picked 36 pounds and on July 8 they picked 56 pounds. Some are sent for sale to the greengrocer.

The walls on which currants, gooseberries, cherries and tayberries are growing have also been netted. Here long metal poles or canes are fixed to the tops of the walls with their feet stuck into the bed below, some distance out from the wall; green nylon netting is fixed over the poles. The walls in this garden do not appear to have ever had any permanent rods, pulleys or hooks attached to the copings so that protective netting could be more easily fixed. This is surprising as the remains of these fixtures can still be seen often in old gardens, even in quite modest ones. They were a useful adjunct to fruit walls from the early nineteenth century onwards; peach walls in particular were sometimes given projecting copings of glass from which nets could be hung, protecting blossom from frost and fruit from birds. Possibly Cottesbrooke did have them once; if so they must have become too dilapidated to use, and were taken away. Doug's newest wall-cherry tree, 'Stella', planted last year, was picked yesterday and yielded 1½ pounds of fruit.

In spite of all the present activity, Doug, as always, is thinking several months ahead. The Top Garden is at last planted with next autumn's, winter's and spring's brassicas. There are late and early cauliflowers, late and early sprouts, calabrese, late and early white and purple broccoli, Savoys, 'January King' cabbages, red cabbages and other cabbages named 'Polonius', 'Rearguard', 'Celtic' and 'Winnigstadt'. (I happened to note in an old gardening magazine that 'Winnigstadt' was one of the finest new cabbages in 1877.) A batch of leeks ('Alma') has been planted beside the 'Giant Winter' leeks. The peas are flourishing. Some are ready for eating now; some will be ready for next month and will be frozen while her ladyship is away in Scotland; others will be ready for eating when she comes back, in September.

The kitchen deliveries are, as usual, as varied as Doug can make them from day to day. At the moment he has twenty-seven different kinds of fruit and vegetable to offer the cook.

ripe gooseberries

Grapes beginning to change colour

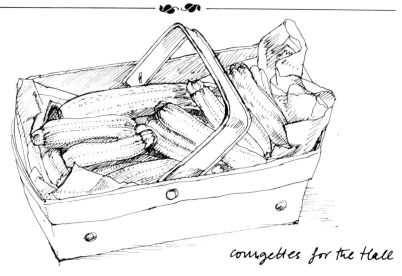

courgettes for the Hall

There are:

baby kohlrabi	summer cauliflowers	salad onions
baby white turnips	celery	Japanese bulb onions
baby beetroots	French beans (last of	cucumbers
baby carrots	the hothouse)	courgettes
peas	cabbages	radishes
broad beans	lettuces	tomatoes
gooseberries	strawberries	tayberries
cherries	figs	red, white, black
raspberries	peaches	currants

This afternoon her ladyship is going to Newmarket for a couple of days, so Doug is packing a small box for the fruit bowl. In it there are: two pounds of strawberries, six figs and six peaches, also some raspberries, red currants and black currants.

The cut flowers are, like the fruit, more varied than ever before; this is a list from Doug's journal of what he has been sending to the Hall for the flower arrangers' vases:

perpetual flowering carnations	pyrethrums
lilies (martagon and hybrid)	cotyledons
geraniums	asparagus fern
delphiniums	yellow scabious (cephalaria)
acidantheras	agapanthus
crassulas	echevarias
sweet Williams	alstroemerias

The pot plants are:

begonias (tuberous and metallica)	gloxinias
golden coleus	achimenes
geraniums (three varieties)	exacums
browallia	small fuchsias

Geraniums in the vinery

Another reminder that gardeners are always thinking months ahead: after discussion with her ladyship Doug has ordered his bulbs for autumn planting. They include 1,550 tulips (500 to be grown for cutting, 300 for forcing and 750 for bedding); 100 hyacinths and 500 narcissi for forcing and 1,000 'assorted bulbs'.

With so much that is new in the way of fruit and vegetables we have rather neglected to look at what is going on in the vinery and potting shed. The grapes are becoming very large; some of the earliest, the 'Madresfield Court', will be ready soon. They have already turned from green to a dark-pinkish blue. Ten days after they finish colouring, Ken tells us, the bloom will start to form and then they will be good for eating. The openings of windows and ventilators in the vinery are covered with fine green mesh, to keep out wasps.

In the potting shed Joy, as always, continues to prick out and pot on or pot up. The 300 cyclamen that arrived at the end of June have been transferred to one-litre pots. She has potted up number-less tuberous and eliator begonias, 600 Dutch begonias, four dozen carnation cuttings, various geraniums and 120 *Primula kewensis*. She has potted on all kinds of herbaceous and perennial rockery seedlings, pricked out six trays of myosotis and several trays of cinerarias, arabis and pansies (60 per box) which were sown earlier this month. Cuttings have been taken of hydrangeas, fuchsias, lemon-scented geranium, *Cupressus funebris* and gold-leaved zonal pelargoniums as well as car-nations. Joy will pot them on in due course. Doug reckons that she must prick out or pot up something like 50,000 bedding plants and 7,000 to 10,000 pot plants in a year.

alstroemerias in a florist's vase

Nor have I mentioned the continual weeding, thinning and watering of seedlings; the spraying of the wall fruit against aphids, of the carnations against fungus and of the vines against red spider; the cleansing of cold frames with Jeyes fluid; the constant disbudding and tying in of the perpetual flowering carnations and the late chrysanthemums (which are now halfway up Jess's canes).

Although there is a lot of work to do, much more in terms of time than there was in the winter, we get the feeling that it is not too difficult; I might (except for the weeding) describe it as easy. The gardeners appear to have everything under control. The days are warm but not too

'Winnigstadt' cabbages and young red cabbages

hot; fruit is setting well and, except for the orchard apples, is prolific. The plastic bags are working wonders as bird scarers, especially the Tesco bags, which have handles on the ends rather than in the middles; Doug has noticed that this makes them aerodynamically better suited to blow about than the Fisons. The only thing that can upset Doug now is rain and absenteeism through sickness. (Unfortunately, by the end of July both are going to try his patience very much indeed.)

Monday, 29 July 1985

Doug and I discuss our next visit on the telephone; he tells me that it has been impossible to pick the outside fruit as often as it should have been picked, as last week the weather was appalling; there is a forecast of more rain to come this week. I tell him it's gales and driving rain here on the Hampshire coast; he says it's the same at Cottesbrooke. He sounds very glum. 'The weeds are higher than the cabbages, and the soft fruit is rotting on the bushes. Neither job can be tackled while the weather stays like this.' As well as Doug's problems with the weather, Jess, having just had ten days of holidays, is still having trouble with his knee and is off sick again.

rain, rain, rain

This makes extra work for the other gardeners, especially for Doug. Jess has actually missed eleven weeks out of a possible twenty so far with his bad knee.

Doug is always courteous, no matter how hard he is pressed, but I hate to add to his burden of work by following him about on a busy day and pestering him with questions. There is also little pleasure in visiting the gardens in filthy weather, but Doug knows that Hugh and I are anxious not to get too behindhand with our record. It seems that the picking of the peaches and the first crop of figs is already finished, they've started on the next crop of nectarines, melons are tumbling out of their safety nets and yesterday the first grapes were sent to the Hall.

Doug thinks we ought to try to come within the next ten days. The weather, whatever it is, has to be recorded in my diary of a year in the gardens at Cottesbrooke. As for Hugh, he has already said on more than one occasion when photographing the gardens that the light after rain is much more beautiful than the light of a hot, sunny day. However, I feel very sorry for Doug. This must be one of the wettest, coldest summers on record. He tempers his despair with sarcasm. 'Well', he says, 'the farm manager and I have decided to give up our normal crops this year. He's going to grow rice and I'm trying watercress.'

(When I came to read Doug's journal for July 29 and 30 all he had written about the weather was 'Rain, rain, rain!' and then 'Rain, rain, bloody rain!')

AUGUST

Twelfth visit Wednesday, 7 August 1985

The weather is still wet and grey; there is also the first hint of autumn in the air. Surely it's very early to be thinking of autumn? Doug agrees, but the signs are there. 'It goes "Ha!" and catches you in the back of the throat in the early morning', he says. Where have I heard this before? It's William Cobbett, writing in 1833, in his *English Gardener*. Actually he was describing greenhouse management in September and he was referring to winter, but the gardener's alertness is the same; 'Ha! we smell winter here.'

The suggestion of autumn is not just in the air: Teresa is piling crisp, dead pea haulms into a wheelbarrow. They belong to the 'Pilot' peas which have all been picked and taken to the kitchen for freezing. I reflect that Cobbett, without a poly tunnel, would have kept those haulms to use as protection for his early peas and beans, his wall-fruit blossom or his artichokes, but here they go to the dump. Then, without even going into the vinery, we can see through the glass that some of the vine leaves are turning from green to yellow.

The melon leaves are also yellowing. The first cucumbers have been cleared from the propagation house and the second crop is being picked in the Top Garden greenhouse. The production of melons in the propagation house shows no sign of slowing down. Some of the 'Tiger' melons have begun to ripen; their pale green stripes with dark-green blotches change to a creamy colour with golden blotches when they are ready. In places where melons have been picked a few safety nets remain, empty and sagging; other previously used nets have been placed under immature melons that are only the size of a croquet ball. The nets hang, stretched and baggy like brassières several sizes too large, waiting to be grown into.

The rain drives us to the shelter of the fruit and vegetable-washing room. There is a little debate going on in here over the best way to pack a large cardboard box. It is being prepared for her ladyship's eldest son, who is visiting the Hall today. Ken, Teresa

melons ripening in their safety nets

and John have lined the box with white paper. A carefully chosen collection of garden produce is lined up on the washroom shelves. The captain is to take it back to his house in Gloucestershire by car. There are:

two heads of celery, freshly picked, washed, trimmed and wrapped
two cucumbers, wrapped like the celery in white paper
a little bunch of spring onions, also washed, trimmed and wrapped
tomatoes in a white plastic punnet
two punnets of nectarines
a large 'Tiger' melon
one punnet of tayberries
three punnets of raspberries
one punnet of morello cherries, labelled 'morello' to avoid confusion
  with dessert cherries
one large wrapped lettuce

The packing is difficult because although the box is large it is also quite deep. By arranging the soft fruit so that nothing will be squashed there is not enough space for the melon and the vegetables. They have tried putting the melon, cucumbers, celery and spring onions in first, but they are so unequal in size that the fruit cannot safely be packed on top without rolling about or tipping up. The last thing to go in is the lettuce which is the size, shape and weight of a football. With the fruit packed as it is at present, it is liable to roll into the raspberries, especially if, as Teresa keeps saying in a worried, fussing way, 'the Captain suddenly puts his foot on the brake.' They try two more arrangements; neither is entirely satisfactory.

Doug appears and confuses everyone by adding a bunch of black grapes and two beautiful green Italian cauliflowers ('Romanesco', sown in the spring and harvested from now until autumn). Everything is taken out of the box again and, with Doug in command, John is sent to find a smaller, squatter box. Doug fits this small box inside the bigger box so that it creates a false bottom and uses the deeper compartment beside it for the vegetables and salad stuff. Quite soon everything is packed again, safely this time. The white lining paper is folded over the top. Even if the Captain steps really violently on the brake, nothing will come to any harm.

After helping to pack the box Teresa turns her attention to the strip where the 'Pilot' peas were growing. She

morello cherry

A collection of Cottesbrooke's summer fruit and vegetables

lightly hoes and rakes it to make it ready for a batch of young curly kale plants. (These are a variety called 'Fribour'.) She checks with Doug on how far apart they should be spaced, mixes a calomel paste to dip the roots into as a safeguard against clubroot and sets to work, planting seven rows; four of seventeen plants, three of fifteen.

In two days' time she will have a few days of holiday. She no longer lives with her parents, both of whom work on the estate. She will probably stay in her lodgings in a nearby village where she lives with her boyfriend. She is saving up to buy a horse which she hopes to take hunting next season. She will have to attend to it before and after work; in the winter, when the days are short, she will exercise it in her lunch hour. She appears to have no hankering for city life, or even for other parts of the country. She is very happy as she is. Until last year she had never seen the sea, and the big shops in the large county town nearby hold no attraction for her.

Teresa is working in the Top Garden. As well as cucumbers, the tomatoes in the Top Garden greenhouse are ready for picking; they share the space with two pretty little plants which are used for cut flowers. One is *Acidanthera muriliae*; the flowers look like single wild white gladioli with purple blotches in their hearts; the other is zephyranthes (also called the Zephyr Lily or the Flower of the West Wind) with delicate flowers like white, pointed-petalled crocuses. Later this month though, as her ladyship will be away, there will be no call for either cut flowers or pot plants for the house.

The black currants outside the green-house have all been picked; the broad beans have 'been blitzed', as Doug says, for their last pods. The only currants yet to be picked are the red currants on the cordoned bushes growing against the west-facing wall of the Middle Garden. They could well remain there in perfect condition until the first frosts, as long as the birds can't get them.

Leaving them on the bushes until the first frosts, or even putting whole branches complete with fruit in the fruit room after the frosts came, was the usual method of keeping currants in the eighteenth and nineteenth centuries. Parson Woodforde wrote in his diary for 12 November 1796, 'We gathered some white currants from a tree in the walled garden this Day about noon.'

Zephyr lilies

Lantern cloches and courgettes under the apple trees

Richard Bradley FRS appears to have had no personal experience of picking his own currants, but he notes a way of retarding them in his *New Improvements of Planting and Gardening* (published in 1720): 'I have known a curious man, when the Fruit has been just ripe, tie up some of the Red Currant Bushes in Mats, to preserve the Fruit upon them 'till August or September, and sometimes later in the year.' He also adds that some gardeners 'plant them against Walls to make the Fruit come larger; but I have never found them half so sweet as the Standards.' The north wall was considered best not only for morello cherries but also for the later currants, raspberries and gooseberries. They were covered with mats or nets as soon as they ripened (usually in August) and periodically checked on dry days for the removal of decaying leaves 'and everything that has a tendency to produce mouldiness, or rottenness' (MacIntosh, 1828).

The rain has spoiled the dahlias and Doug has still not been able to tackle the weeds that now tower over his cabbages. His summer pruning is also delayed. It has been cold and wet since mid-July, but the sweet peas are unaffected; their flowers look brilliant, especially on a grey day. The row is some 30 feet long and six feet high. They were grown from a collection of 12 different colours and 12 different colours are identifiable; they range from darkest crimson and purple through lilac, lavender and vermilion to the palest pink, creamy white and pure white. Some are pale pink or white, edged with a darker colour.

In the Middle Garden the runner beans are flowering almost as prolifically as the sweet peas (they were, after all, introduced by the English botanist Tradescant in the seventeenth century as flowering plants), but none has yet formed pods big enough to pick. The major tasks here have been weeding where possible and the thinning of carrots, fennel, endive and chicory. The first outdoor French beans have been picked, seven weeks after the first forced ones were picked in the vinery.

By mid-afternoon the rain has increased and a gale is blowing. The sliding door at the eastern end of the poly tunnel is closed against the draught. I push it open to get inside for the tunnel's protection. Sweet, warm moist air gushes out; it's like a cow's breath. Once inside, my reading spectacles and camera lens mist up. Capsicums and aubergines are growing well, with fruit almost ready to pick. The 'Ogen' melons are already the size of tennis balls; they will ripen when the propagation house melons have finished. There are cucumbers here, and self-blanching celery. The tomatoes are recovering their equilibrium after the disaster with the manure affected by weedkiller. In the spaces left by the early

Ripe 'Peregrine' peaches

aubergines starting to flower

peas and beans Doug has tried a late, experimental sowing of a French bean ('Sunray'). He has also sown more carrots, more parsley and more radishes. The Chinese gooseberries are beginning to fruit. Outside the tunnel the lettuces are finished. They have been replaced by eighty-four 'January King' cabbages

August brings another spate of seed-sowing for Doug. For the last four minutes he has been mixing and sieving 12½ bushels of 6-pound seed compost. I ask him what '6-pound compost' means; he explains that 6 pounds of fertiliser goes into every 12½ bushels of compost. This compost (a soil-less one made up of nine secret ingredients) was mixed for 23 packets of exotic greenhouse plant seed. The list, for an amateur like myself, is incomprehensible. Sometimes a common name exists; where it does I have put it in brackets.

> *Alpinia speciosa (Indian shell flower)*
> *Alpinia formosana*
> *Solanum auriculatum*
> *Thunbergia fragrans (Clock vine)*
> *Podalyria sericea*
> *Achasma megalocheilos*
> *Duranta repens*
> *Casesalpinia gilliesii*
> *Cordia sebestena*
> *Plumeria rubra hybrids (Frangipani or West Indian jasmine)*
> *Leea coccinea*
> *Lantana camara (Wayfaring tree)*
> *Justicia betonica*

Erodia ridleyi
Costus zebrinus
Canagga odorata
Iochroma coccinea
Hedychium spicatum (Indian garland flower)
Hymenosporum flavum
Elettaria cardamomum (Cardamum plant)
Anigozanthus rufus (Kangaroo paw)
Anigozanthus flavidus (Kangaroo paw)

In the kitchens up at the Hall the cook and her assistant, Vanessa, a 17-year-old from the village with a punk hair-cut, are freezing a batch of broad beans and *petits pois* from the gardens. The quantities of Doug's produce which have already been canned, bottled, frozen or made into jam, are colossal; they need to be to see this large household through a winter like the last one, when fresh garden supplies were so badly affected by the weather.

The workings of the kitchen do not concern us here, but with meals for her ladyship, her occasional visitors and guests, and meals for the resident staff it is not difficult to see how the box-loads of garden produce sent daily by Doug are consumed. The day's menu is discussed between the butler and the cook every morning after breakfast; the butler then proposes the menu to her ladyship for her approval. By 10am he has told Doug what's wanted. This is also the moment for Doug to tell the butler if there is anything special in the gardens that day. By midday Doug's order is delivered to the kitchen, neatly packed, trimmed, cleaned and, if necessary, washed.

summer-time preserves

S E P T E M B E R

Thirteenth visit Thursday, 5 September 1985

Another early start for Hugh and me, as we must be at Cottesbrooke before today's two boxes of fruit, flowers and vegetables are dispatched to Scotland. They have to be ready for the 11.30 am train to Inverness. We saw on our last visit how tricky the packing of fruit and vegetables can be, with the box intended for the Captain. Doug doesn't risk sending soft fruit by train to Scotland but he does send melons, nestling them in runner beans for protection. We want a photograph of this, it sounds so ingenious, though to tell the truth we are going to have to cheat by bringing Doug a bought melon of the 'Blenheim Orange' kind. He told us on the telephone yesterday that the only melon worth sending from the gardens with this consignment is one small 'Emerald Gem', which will look rather insignificant all on its own in a huge box of runner beans. The Cottesbrooke 'Blenheim Orange' melons are finished; this is the last of the 'Emerald Gems'. The poly tunnel's 'Ogens' are just starting to ripen, but none is ready yet for what Doug describes in his journal as today's 'onward transmission to Scotland'.

He gives a smug grunt as he picks the price label (109p) and the label of its place of origin (Israel) from our Marks and Spencer melon. He cradles it beside the 'Emerald Gem' in a big square wooden box which is already lined with newspaper and runner beans. Hugh takes a photograph; Doug removes our melon and continues to fill the box. The 'Emerald Gem' is joined by some green peppers and aubergines from the poly tunnel and a few courgettes from the lantern cloches. More beans go on top with another sheet of newspaper; then Doug begins a new layer of beans on top of which go cooking apples, dessert apples ('Worcester Pearmains'), white carrots (grown from the French seed I gave him in the spring), two cucumbers, a bunch of carnations wrapped in tissue paper and six trimmed Florence fennels. Each of the fennels is wrapped in tissue to contain their anise-smell; this is very strong as they have just been taken from the garden. The carrots have also just been dug up and, like the fennels, they have been washed,

melons for Scotland and washed white carrots

Florence Fennel

trimmed and wrapped by Teresa. Tissue paper goes over this layer which reaches the top of the box. Doug adds a letter to the butler which reads: 'Tom! these are white carrots the other odd veg is Florence fennel. Cook like celery. Apples are cooking and dessert. Doug.' We have been here since 8.45 am. It is raining. There is blue smoke climbing slowly out of the bungalow chimney in the corner of the Middle Garden and there is no doubt of it being autumn on this visit. It is so grey and cold that it feels more like October. In early October we will have completed our year here. It seems as if we have already been full circle, although there is the rest of September still to come. We feel like this because the vinery is beginning to look as it did on our first visit. The tomatoes have been cut down; the leaves are beginning to fall from the peach and nectarine trees, the next crop of figs (the third and last) is beginning to form. Pot plants have been brought in here again; clivias and arum lilies, strelizias, pelargoniums and standard fuchsias.

The melon house is changing too. It is now stripped of melons and cucumbers and is about to become a propagation house again. The washed, sprayed and disinfected grey slate bench tops stand empty, waiting for a new set of seeds, cuttings and seedlings. The frames are packed with infant cinerarias, baby begonias and juvenile cyclamen. The 'Summer Cloud' has been washed off the glass and the polythene shades have been taken down in the greenhouses. There are large mounds of sand, ashes and spent compost by the box shed. These are the ingredients for the plunge bed for the pots containing forcing bulbs – hyacinths, tulips, narcissi and daffodils – that will form part of her ladyship's décor next Christmas and next spring. The first bulbs to be forced will be hyacinths and narcissi for Christmas. They will be buried, in pots, in about ten days' time. By the end of the month the bulbs ordered in July – hundreds of narcissi, tulips, hyacinths and daffodils – will have followed suit; these will be flowering in her ladyship's drawing rooms in early spring.

The trick of forcing the hardier kinds of bulbs in a plunge bed has been practised by gardeners for centuries. The beds could be made of any clean, dense but light material; MacIntosh (1828) recommends rotten tan, sawdust or dry light mould. Bulbs were also forced in heated frames or hothouses but the advantage of a plunge bed, as MacIntosh points out, is that 'because it excludes the action of air, a disposition is naturally brought on to push out roots; and these being once produced in abundance, there can be little doubt that the bloom will be proportionably stronger'.

Ken and John have had their summer holiday; they spent a week with the rest of the family in a caravan near Cromer and were lucky with the weather, mysteriously, as most of England has had rain every day during August.

Ken is picking bunches of grapes for the second box to go to Scotland. The vinery has just been fumigated and smells strongly of tobacco. There are wasps in here all the same, nipping in and out of gaps in the roof where panes of glass have slipped. Here and there they have demolished whole bunches. Ken cuts the grapes so that they retain a piece of woody, T-shaped stem, which means that he severs the branch from which they hang each time he takes a bunch; he therefore cuts the first bunches from the furthest end of each shoot. Like everything else he does, he works carefully and slowly, trimming off the yellowing leaves that come with each bunch, as they would taint the fruit by going mouldy in the box. Today he needs two 'Madresfield Courts', two 'Buckland Sweet-waters' and two 'Black Hamburghs'. He picks the black grapes when they are at their darkest, without a hint of pink, and the white ones when their green turns to yellow. He washes them at the wash-room sink to rid them of the fumigator spray. The water, repelled by their bloom, rolls off them, leaving them pretty well dry. He is very careful not to spoil the bloom, holding them always by the T-shaped stem and snipping out any damaged or bad berries with his sharp pointed vine scissors. Each bunch is then patted quite dry with a tea-towel and wrapped in tissue paper.

The second box is a new one, made by the estate carpenter. Before it can be sent to Scotland Doug must paint a black, open umbrella on it to show which is the right way up.

The first box has been finished off with more paper and wood-wool packing. The lid has been nailed down and the address printed on the lid by Doug with 'This way up please. Urgent. With care. TBCF. Inverness'. Ken ties it up securely with string from an enormous ball held by John. There are four people in this tiny room. Ken, John and Teresa are all helping Doug to pack the second box. First goes a sheet of newspaper, then a layer of apples; this is covered in more newspaper, then in go two plastic punnets of gages ('Count d'Authann'), two punnets of 'Victoria' plums and two punnets of tomatoes. It is decided to tip the tomatoes in loose, to make more space. Then go more carnations, trimmed and wrapped in tissue paper by Teresa; more tissue paper is crumpled on top. 'White!' calls Doug. 'Not pink. Pink stains if it gets wet.' Lastly we have Ken's six bunches of grapes and more tissue paper. Then come wood-wool, the lid, nails, string, address. Doug fills in a packing note, '2 boxes of fresh fruit and veg', and Ken is sent straight away with them to the station, picking up the money for their freight from the estate office on his way. It is now about 9.30am.

Outside there are wasps everywhere. Hunters on early exercise clip-clop by down the lane. The grass has been mown in the orchard, ready for the apple picking. Ladders lean on the walls where the plums and gages have been picked, but except for the 'Worcesters' the other kinds of apple are only just starting to colour. It is a bad year for apples. The best crop will come from one ancient tree, a 'Monarch', which is loaded with fruit. It is illuminated against the tree's dark-green leaves by the reflecton of the sun which comes out at midday; light bounces off the shiny mown grass below the tree and gives the apples a pale-green glow.

There is a late crop of strawberries, some of the outdoor peaches have been picked, blackberries are ripe in the fruit cage, and the late raspberries ('Leo') have grown so high they hit the top netting. The curly endive is fully grown and ready for blanching; the fennel is in fine feather, literally, the line of white bulbs has a mass of thick dark-green fronds waving above it. The onions have also done well and are lying in rows on the ground, to dry off if possible.

The sweet peas are still flowering prolifically and the winter celery in trenches is ready to be tied and earthed up. But Doug has had problems with his early Brussels sprouts. They are 'blowing', instead of buttoning, because of too much rain. He has also dug up the Chinese gooseberries in the tunnel. They were not a great success – not enough sun. The lack of sun has also affected his corn cobs, which began so bravely but have hardly grown at all. The same goes for the courgettes, which are growing so slowly that they still have the protection of their cloches. The parsnips are also very poor. Everything is at least three weeks late because of the weather, though Doug has been able to start lifting his main crop potatoes; the main crop carrots are nearly ready too. A great barrow of pink potatoes ('Vanessa') waits in the tunnel, out of the rain, for John to deal with. He is sent to make storage bays for them in one of the old out-houses, using straw bales. 'Vanessas' are earlies and will be used first. The main crop will go in a clamp, as it

Onions drying off before lifting

onions drying off

did last year.

In the tunnel, the space left by the removal of the Chinese gooseberries is being dug for winter lettuces. They will be 'Miranda' and 'Mayfair' again, the same as last year. Once again Doug is thankful for the tunnel. His experimental sowing of French beans is proving a success as they are about to flower. The 'Ogen' melons are flourishing, with five or six fruits to a plant. The aubergines and peppers are still cropping, also a delicious orange tomato, 'Tangella'. The first batch of self-blanching celery is finished and a new crop is coming on.

The biggest problem at the moment is the weeding. The third and last Open Day of the year is in ten days' time, but the weather has made hoeing and weeding impossible; a little hoeing was done this Monday in the nursery area reserved for next year's bedding out plants and the weeds are already growing up again. The Top Garden is worst; sow-thistles flourish among the brassicas. Doug plans to keep the visitors out of it with a wattle hurdle across the entrance. He has been even more anxious than usual about Open Day since he has heard that a coachload of about fifty kitchen garden and allotment enthusiasts from a nearby city is to be expected, as well as the normal visitors. He is awfully worried that the gardens won't be up to his usual standard, but at last he has Jess back at work, and among the red cabbages there are several that must weigh 12 pounds at least. Jess himself is, as usual, disbudding his chrysanthemums and tying up his carnations. He plans to give up the postman's job in October and work here full time. Sid is here today, to help with the hoeing.

Joy is, as usual, in the potting shed, working today on pot upon pot of orchids which need tying up with green raffia and supporting with slender canes. She says she really likes long, boring jobs that she can get stuck into. She asks me if I knew that the building attached to the southern end of the almshouses was once the village school, which I didn't. It was built by the tenth Langham baronet in 1813, for forty-eight village children, which seems incredible as it is not much bigger than a modern two-car garage. On the site of the rubbish dump, just outside the potting shed, there used to be a cottage for the schoolteacher (whom the tenth baronet paid £30 a year). Within living memory the cottage was still inhabited by a schoolteacher, who taught up to twenty-three children aged from 5 to 14 in one class, in that tiny school. Joy's informant, herself once a child at that school and later a schoolteacher too, is the daughter of the late estate blacksmith. Apparently, after prayers, the day always began with the whole school reciting 'The Lady of Shallot'.

I have also discovered something about the strange sundial in the centre of the Middle Garden. It is definitely Edwardian and was originally placed in the centre of the parterre in a walled garden up at the Hall. It was possibly designed by the

orchids

'Vanessa' potatoes waiting to be stored

architect, Robert Weir Schultz, who is known to have designed the Hall gardens between 1911 and 1914. The only thing that puzzles me now is the origin of its sad little verses. There is a different one engraved on each of its four faces. On the north face it says: 'Beyond the tomb fresh flowers bloom.' On the south face: 'Amidst the flowers I tell the hours.' On the east face: 'Time wanes away as flowers decay' and on the west face: 'So man shall rise above the skies.' I can't help wondering if the west face ought to be facing east in view of those words.

Ken returns from the station at about 10.30am. The two boxes cost £11.97 to send to Scotland. It is difficult not to comment on the anomaly or anachronism of a situation in which, in 1985, a total of 13 kilos of home-grown runner beans, a melon, tomatoes, plums, cucumbers, dessert grapes, fennels, white carrots, cooking and dessert apples, gages, peppers, aubergines, courgettes and carnations is packed into two home-made boxes with as much care as if the contents were a set of Meissen porcelain. The boxes are then sent 400 miles by train, for ultimate delivery to a house which is only fifteen miles from the station at Inverness; a town that is not ill-supplied with shops that could probably provide all those items, with the exception of the white carrots. The shop fruit and vegetables might possibly not be so well grown or so fresh, but they would certainly cost less. As a garden historian, however, I am delighted, thrilled to find that this situation at Cottesbrooke exists. It is a continuation of a tradition which is as old, almost, as kitchen

Jess thinning lettuces
by the sundial

gardening itself. The staff at home always sent fruit, flowers, vegetables, herbs and pot plants to the owner as well as game, meat, eggs and dairy produce whenever he or she was staying at any of his or her other houses. This was especially useful, before the advent of reliable butchers, dairies or greengrocers' shops, if the family had moved to town for a month or two. There was also the comfort, with possibly a touch of what Doug would call 'the kudos', of being able to eat at a table laden with the same wholesome food as one was accustomed to at home. The habit of sending hampers of garden produce by train to London certainly continued into the 1930s, when whole families would leave their country estates and spend the best part of summer in town for 'the Season'. As soon as the grouse shooting began, on August 12, shooting parties would leave for Yorkshire or Scotland and the hampers would follow them there.

Old gardening books gave considerable space to instructions on how to pack fruit, in particular, for sending away. In 1699 George London and Henry Wise, nurserymen and gardeners to all the royalty and nobility of England in their time, edited a translation by John Evelyn of *The Complete Gardener* by Jean de la Quintinye, gardener at Versailles to Louis XIV. Transport itself was quite a problem. 'Hard baking Pears and Apples may be laid "pell mell" in Baskets and can be carried by Horse and Cart', they wrote, 'but we cannot do so with tender mellow Pears when they are ripe . . . they are like the Figs, and Peaches &c their delicacy and tenderness requires a gentle usage, like Beautiful young Ladies, otherwise the agitation of the Carriage would bruise and blacken them . . .' Such fruit, they say, should have 'water Carriage, or the Back or Arms of a Porter without any jogging'. De la Quintinye's peaches were laid in a moss-lined cloth, stem end down and wrapped in vine leaves. The last layer was covered with leaves, then the cloth was wrapped over and well fastened. Grapes could be sent in the same way as peaches or packed in cases with bran. Figs were sent in sieves two inches deep, packed in single layers with leaves above and below. Paper was sewn on top 'to keep the fruit close'. Plums could be sent in a basket with leaves or nettles laid below and above them to preserve the bloom, then covered with linen cloth or paper. 'Common Plums may be sent in Bigger Baskets.'

By the beginning of the nineteenth century, transport, both on land and by water, had speeded up to such an extent that baskets were no longer considered suitable for the carriage of fruit. 'It is liable to be injured by being bruised', wrote MacIntosh in 1828 (the coaching era was in its hey-day, and the railway age was just

tomatoes, aubergines, peppers

beginning). 'Boxes of tin or deal should be used for this purpose, and of sizes according to the quantity to be sent.' The boxes, if of wood, were to be made of inch-thick deal, 'secured at the corners with iron clamps, and secured with locks, each lock having two keys, one to be kept by the person who packs the fruit, and the other by the person who unpacks it'.

Criticism of the wisdom of employing several gardeners to produce fruit and vegetables at home when garden stuff can be bought more cheaply in the shops is not unfamiliar to the garden historian either. As long ago as 1837, the year before a committee was formed to look into the economics of the young Queen Victoria's kitchen gardens, Loudon, as editor of *The Gardener's Magazine*, was urging that the kitchen gardens at Kensington Palace should be scrapped, partly because they were unproductive, being on gravelly ground, but also because: 'It is now just as easy to purchase pineapples and melons . . . from the London shops, as it is to purchase apples or oranges: witness the numbers that are produced on the occasion of any public dinner.'

Doug is enormously proud of what he is doing in the gardens at Cottesbrooke, but that does not mean that he necessarily condones the great expense of running them as they are run at present. He actually tries to reduce running costs as much as possible. He is also ferociously protective of his domain. Like all good gardeners, he is constantly on the look-out for predators, both feathered and human. There is scaffolding at the moment on Doug's house where one of his chimneys is being mended by the estate. He went up last week to look at the view and had a grand spectacle of his Top and Middle Gardens, his frame yard and his orchard. 'I could see little patches of red jersey too, flitting about between the trees in the orchard. I said to myself "There's something down there that shouldn't be!"' It was a gang of village children scrumping apples. Doug came rushing down the ladder, sprinted across the gardens and gave them a ticking off they'll not forget for a long time. 'Worst thing of it though', he says, 'is that they weren't actually *eating* the apples, they were just *throwing* them.'

Hugh and I plan to surprise Doug with our next visit by coming to the Open Day.

Fourteenth visit Sunday, 15 September 1985

As if to make up for all the trouble it has given over the past few weeks the weather on Open Day is lovely and sunny. For the third and last time this year Doug has distributed fly-posters to all the local village halls, church notice-boards and pubs, spruced up the gardens and placed his signboards at appropriate points in the park and gardens. Once again Joy and the village ladies have made cakes, scones, biscuits and sandwiches, and have laid out the Open Day chairs and tables in the laundry yard. The gardens are open in aid of 'the Nurses', from 2 till 6 pm. By the time I arrive, this time with friends from nearby, there is a mass of cars in a specially designated space under the shade of the park trees. They have been directed up the drive and over the hump-backed bridge by the ticket-man at the lodge gates. Entrance is 50p for an adult, 25p for a child.

The wild gardens, water gardens, formal gardens and laundry yard are filled with people. Whole families are out for the day, sitting or strolling, admiring the gigantic park trees, the beautiful topiary work, the mown and smoothly striped lawns, the weed-free shrubberies and herbaceous borders, the ornamental stone urns brimming over with flowers.

Joy stands beaming behind another kind of urn in the Old Laundry – a tea-urn. Here the village ladies' cakes and scones, many of which are filled with real cream, are being bought up at a great pace. It is now 4 o'clock and it looks likely that the cakes will soon be finished, and we therefore settle down for tea. My friends have been very much impressed by the gardens so far; 'Quite the best we've ever seen in this county', they tell me. I feel as proud as if I owned them myself.

There is a distinctly festive air to the place today; everyone is on holiday, even the gardeners; everyone that is, except Hugh, who is hard at work. He appears in the laundry yard, and rejects tea as he is still taking photographs. He is accompanied by John in smart weekend clothes with a camera of his own slung round his neck. It is John's turn to ask Hugh's advice now, on photography.

I have saved the kitchen gardens till last for my friends to look at. We make our way across the park. It is windy and still sunny; behind us the Hall sparkles with its golden weathercock, pink brick and spotless windows. The shutters are up as her ladyship is still away. A flock of wild geese flies in a V across the tops of the trees, honking. They had been swimming on the lake until someone scared them off. It glitters, pale blue, surrounded by the light green of the park pasture. We walk towards the kitchen gardens

ripening plums
('Coe's Golden Drop')

along the route of the old drive; it is now as grassy as the rest of the park, but it is still discernible as a wide raised track, curving towards the lake and the original, three-arched stone bridge. We walk through the orchard towards the ornamental iron gateway that leads into the Middle Garden. Doug and Ken are just inside the gateway, the former is very much at ease in a tie-less weekend shirt, suede jerkin, brown trousers and moccasins, the latter is almost standing at attention. He wears a smart tweed cap instead of his usual old working cap, a blue blazer with brass buttons, new jeans and, in place of the white tennis shoes that he wears every day to work in, soft, pale leather boots.

There are crowds of people here. Children eye the plums and peaches on the walls, and the strawberries and cordoned apples lining the paths. Their mothers peer closely at the vegetables, especially the rhubarb, fennel and courgettes. No doubt they are comparing the progress here with that of their own kitchen gardens at home. Two old gardeners make their way very slowly round the Middle Garden poking at plants with their walking sticks, checking everything. They read all the labels, they notice the blown sprouts, the fine carrots, the oversized beetroots ('Had too much rain'), the length or lack of it of the runner beans, the size of the cabbages, the red currants still hanging on the cordoned bushes on the walls, the placing of the leeks (they know Doug's predecessor always used this very same leek bed), the swedes coming on, the magnitude of the potato crop. They approve on the whole. 'He's improved the place a lot', says one to the other. The onions have all been lifted since we were here last, and the weeding is immaculate. Doug is glowing with pride at the compliments he receives. He says many of the visitors today are regulars, particularly the two old gardeners who are now making their way into the frame yard; many more visitors are newcomers though, as this Open Day was mentioned in one of the national dailies as well as on local radio.

Ken and Doug have been besieged all afternoon with people asking them horticultural questions. At the same time they are keeping an eye out for predators; they are well-positioned here, with views of the frame yard, orchard and Middle Garden. Doug has closed off the Top Garden with a wattle fence and fastened nets over the open doors at each end of the tunnel.

In the frame yard the vinery range and propagation house are prudently locked; so is the fruit room, Doug's office, the potting shed, mushroom house and mess room. People drift in and out of the houses that have been left open, dazzled by the gloxinias in the palm house, and the mass of pink, white and red gesnerias in

Doug and Ken on Open Day

the stove house, checking the temperatures, ogling the grapes. Children run giggling from end to end of Jess's rows of chrysanthemums which have grown almost to the tops of their canes so that they form a long, tall, narrow green passageway.

This is a very successful day for Doug. About 500 people have visited the gardens. By evening he is preening like a turkey-cock. He's had so many well-deserved compliments, so much rapt admiration. 'You see now why it's such hard work before they come?' We do. He lets us into a secret about the stripes on the lawns. They were not made by the mower, as it broke down just when it was most wanted. To make the grass look mown, Doug ran rollers over it this morning.

propagation, palm, carnation
and stove houses

OCTOBER

Fifteenth and last visit Thursday, 3 October 1985

This is the last visit we shall make as the recorders of a year in the kitchen gardens at Cottesbrooke. Our first visit was almost exactly a year ago, on 8 October 1984. We began coming here the week after the gardeners had sent their annual contribution to the church for the Harvest Festival. Today they are literally polishing and grooming the fruit, flowers and vegetables for this year's Harvest Festival, which is on Sunday, in three days' time.

We also want to take a group photograph; Doug has made sure that everyone will be here this morning. There is a gale blowing, it's raining a little, it's grey and damp. Doug has wrenched his knee; he tripped over the pipes in the vinery. Joy has 'flu. Nevertheless, the whole of the kichen garden staff is present. We begin by posing them outside while the rain is still only slight, choosing a corner by the mushroom house and a flower bed made bright with dahlias and petunias.

Sid is in his cap and bright-blue boiler suit; Jess is as usual without a cap, in a dark-blue boiler suit; John wears jeans, T-shirt and anorak; Teresa is well wrapped up in her waxed cotton Barbour; Ken has on his old working cap, tweed jacket, jeans and tennis shoes; Doug wears a tweed jacket, flat cap and tie; the cap and tie were brought to the gardens at the last minute from the house by Joy, who is well muffled up in a track suit and a padded anorak. She holds Rodney in her arms.

The rain increases. It seems best to move the whole party to the vinery. Doug sits on the vinery step ladder; Joy still nurses the cat; Sid stares stoically ahead, arms straight down by his sides; John is blinking; Teresa and Ken are slightly less ill at ease than the rest; Jess is visibly thinking that this is all a very silly waste of time. He is now fully employed here, having retired from his postman's job after twenty-five years. This long service entitles him to a presentation of two mementoes of his choice, one for his wife and one for himself. He has chosen a clock and a sewing machine. The presentation takes place at the post office tomorrow. He is very nervous as he will have to make a public speech of thanks. All Joy and Teresa can say is, 'What'll we do without the rubber bands?' He collects them from the bundles of letters on his round.

The group photograph is taken and everyone is released into what has become a drizzle again. It's the first rain for four weeks, after the longest dry spell this summer. The gardens are beginning to look wintry. The canes have been taken from the sweet peas which are dead or dying and tumbled down; their leaves are brown and only a few blooms remain. Sid doggedly continues to clear the brassica ground beside the sweet peas, digging out old cabbage stumps with the well-practised, minimal pressure of the experienced gardener's boot on the fork. Sixty years of gardening have taught him how to work hard and steadily, without wasteful over-exertion. He wheels each barrow-load of old stumps to the dump. The rubbish is cleared from time to time by a farm tractor and used to fill holes elsewhere on the estate.

Most of the main crop potatoes, the 'Edzell Blues', 'Pink Fir Apples', 'Caras', 'Draytons', 'Romanos' and 'Crofts', are dug up now. Some of them are waiting in a heap on a bed of straw covered by a plastic sheet, to be clamped. This year's clamp is to be in the Top Garden, where the peas and broad beans were growing. After today's rain Doug hopes the ground will be damp enough to start building it.

The celery trenches have been earthed up, making long neat ridges with ditches between them; the dark-green tops of the celery poke out along the spines of the ridges. The nursery bed of forget-me-nots and wallflowers has been raided by the Hall gardeners for the planting of their springtime flower beds. The tying up and disbudding of the lines of winter-flowering chrysanthemums continues, almost daily. The plants are now taller than me, and I'm 5 foot 6 inches tall. They will soon be moved into the vinery. The reason for the disbudding has been puzzling me for weeks. Doug explains that each plant is intended to produce no more than eight blooms, but these will be gigantic, the size of a large grapefruit and mop-shaped. He has read somewhere that each flower grown in this manner will have 374 petals. The border next to the winter chrysanthemums is filled with smaller, less tortured chrysanthemums, all flowering now; pink, orange, yellow, white and brown. There are still a few outdoor flowers, gladioli and dahlias, to cut for the house, but the rest, the lilies, delphiniums and sweet peas, are over. The gardeners will be cutting hothouse flowers again, quite soon.

In the fruit room and wash house the fruit, flowers and vegetables for the Harvest Festival are being assembled. Everything was picked or dug up early this morning before we came, and is now being washed, trimmed, buffed up and, if appropriate, tied tidily with raffia. The vegetables, in particular, are being dressed up as if they were about to be entered in a horticultural competition. One of the greatest pleasures of my childhood was the village and county flower and produce shows, in which both amateur and professional gardeners could compete. Sadly, these events, if they are held at all, are now nothing like what they used to be. Prompted by the sight of several First Prize cards from the county show and a framed, illuminated notice hanging in his office which said 'exhibited by Her Ladyship', I did ask Doug, earlier in the year, if there were any local horticultural shows and if so, did he compete in them? The answer to both questions was no; the village flower show no longer took place, and even if it did there would be no one else in the professional's class for Doug to compete against.

For the Harvest Festival there are bunches of spray chrysanthemums, gladioli, orchids, carnations and red and white geraniums standing in tin flower vases. There are three varieties of potatoes – pink 'Vanessas', yellow 'Draytons' and violet 'Edzell Blues' – all scrubbed and arranged in sieves; there are two varieties of tomato, orange and red, in a box with glossy purple aubergines and shining red and green peppers; there is one bunch of white grapes and one bunch of black with some Worcester apples in another box. This is lined with bright-pink tissue paper. There's another box containing bright-green cooking apples. There are two red cabbages with the bloom still on them, and two 'Winnigstadt', their veined leaves curled to a pouting point so that each cabbage looks like a huge green rosebud. There are four cauliflowers, white curds fringed with pointed green leaflets. Twelve round white turnips have been tied in bunches of three; their stems and leaves are left on to add to their decorative appearance. The same has been done to six swedes, beets both cylindrical and spherical, carrots both orange and white; all are washed spotless. Onions, loose skin picked off, are tied by their necks in bunches of three; leeks have their green flags left full length, but they are folded back and neatly tied with raffia; they remind me of the way the tails of cart-horses are tied up at ploughing matches. Self-blanching celery has also had its leaves left on; its stems are bound with raffia. The fennels' stems have been cut longer than usual in order to leave a fair bit of stalk and feather. The last of the figs lie head to tail on a bed of their own leaves. Finally there are two enormous marrows, courgettes that have been allowed to grow full size especially for this occasion.

onions for the Harvest Festival

The plan is to take all this bounty into the vinery so that Hugh can photograph it. We don't have any clear idea of how it should be arranged, beyond keeping it clean by covering the bare earth where it is to be laid out with sheets of newspaper. Ken, watched by the usual fruit-packing committee of Doug, Teresa and John, quite naturally and easily takes charge of the display. It turns out that Ken has an uncle who was a greengrocer and florist; he works as if he habitually made arrangements for shop windows or the show bench or indeed the Harvest Festival, placing the flowers at the back, the brassicas in the centre, celery and sieves of potatoes either side and the smaller, less leafy stuff in front with the fruit in the foreground. The newspaper, with its Fleet Street cheesecake, half-finished crosswords, racing results and scandalous headlines, is gradually covered by all this innocent fruitfulness. The whole arrangement is set up within half an hour. Hugh photographs it, then it is all dismantled. 'Take it to the church, Ken', orders Doug adding (for our benefit), 'That's the best place to keep this sort of stuff you know; somewhere cold and damp.' Some of the people in the village will contribute garden produce as well, but no one, Doug thinks, will have bigger marrows than his, this year. Those who don't grow vegetables will send canned beans, he says, or whatever they think is suitable. The church arrangements will not be done by Doug or Ken, but by the village ladies.

The knowledge that we will not be coming here any more, at least not as regularly as we have been over the past year, makes us both very sad. We look at the potting shed for the last time. Jess is pruning the potted stan- dard fuchsias. They have been brought in from the courtyard in the Hall gardens and are about to take up their winter quarters again in the Top Garden greenhouse. He makes

carrots for the Harvest Festival

Ken, Teresa, Joy and Rodney, John, Jess, Sid and Doug (seated)

cuttings from the trimmings, stripping the lowest leaves from the stems, dipping the stems in rooting powder then pushing them deeply into pots of sandy rooting compost. Fuchsias for the future, I think, feeling as if the wheel has turned full circle, but it's a carousel on which I've had my turn.

Outside the potting shed, the plunge bed bristles with thin, labelled canes. Each cane marks a buried box or pot of bulbs. Each label bears the date of burial and the variety of bulb. The bulbs will be moved into a hothouse in due course, when Doug judges the time to be right. Each pot or box is sprinkled with a layer of yellow sand before it gets buried so that when the gardeners dig down for them they'll know when to stop. It seems odd that I took no notice of this quite important adjunct to winter-flowering pot plants when I first came here a year ago, but my attention was taken entirely at that time by fruit and vegetables.

There is still one regular occurrence that I've not yet properly described. This is the weekly replenishment of the flowers on the family's grave. Sometimes her ladyship does this herself, sometimes Doug or Ken do it, but once a week it has to be done, usually on a Friday. This week, a day early, Doug picks some smallish chrysanthemums from the border in the frame yard. Teresa adds some asparagus fern from her palm house. Doug fills an old plastic lemonade bottle with fresh water and because of his knee we drive to the graveyard just the other side of the road from the gardens. Although the family has lived in Cottesbrooke for over fifty years there is only one grave in the family plot. The gravestone is simple, a replica, Doug says, of Sir Winston Churchill's. He takes last week's roses, now wilted, from a green, fluted florist's vase with spiked feet. It stands on a little patch of neatly clipped grass set into the gravestone. He pours out the old water, pours fresh water in from the plastic bottle, arranges the fern and chrysanthemums and limps back to his van at the gate.

long beets

Overhead, low-flying FIII jets, AIO tank-busters and transport planes are once again on exercise. I have noticed them on previous visits. They are painted black and are ugly. They smack and zip at a terrific speed through the low clouds over the Hall. They come from as far away as Suffolk, Doug says, and they use the Hall as a reference mark for their training flights. The noise is

Harvest Festival; fruit, flowers and vegetables

sudden, deafening and frightening. Sheep graze unconcernedly in the field next to the churchyard. The village street beyond is out of sight, hidden by the trees on a bend in the road. Inside the dignified parish church behind us is the tomb of Alderman Langham who bought the manor of Cottesbrooke in 1638 and was the grandfather of the Langham who built the Hall.

It is really very difficult not to feel sentimental, in the original sense of the word, about the fact that this is the day of our last visit. As we watched the gardeners prepare their Harvest Festival offering we were aware, not for the first time, of the pride and pleasure which they take in their work. We were also conscious, as we have been right from the start, of the great respect they have for their employer. Furthermore, although they all deny that they are in the least bit religious, they do revere their local church. Had I not visited the graveyard it might not have occurred to me to add that they also seemed to have, as I suppose all gardeners do, a particular respect for life and death.

It is unlikely that these kitchen gardens will be kept going as they are now, when it comes to the turn of the next generation of the family that owns them. It is sad that 350 years of tradition will come to an end, but it is some consolation that I was able to record how it was, for one year at least.

FINIS